INDIE AUTHOR CONFIDENTIAL 4

SECRETS NO ONE WILL TELL YOU ABOUT WRITING

M.L. RONN

ABOUT THIS SERIES

This isn't your typical writing self-help book. This series is a compilation of lessons learned from an indie author trying to walk the path to success. Follow author M.L. Ronn (Michael La Ronn) as he navigates what it means to master the craft of writing, marketing, and running a profitable publishing business. Learn from his successes and failures, and learn about things that most successful authors only talk about behind the scenes.

To read all the collected volumes of this series in an anthology, visit www.authorlevelup.com/confidential.

CONTENTS

BECOME A TECHNOLOGY-DRIVEN WRITER

BECOME A DATA-DRIVEN WRITER

BECOME THE WRITER OF THE FUTURE

IDEAS YOU CAN STEAL

INTRODUCTION

This volume covers the first quarter of 2021, a new year and hopefully much better than 2020!

It's refreshing to start a new year and put my new strategy into action.

The last volume was decidedly marketing-focused. I concluded both my "Beast Mode" and "Amnesia Mode" challenges, racking up a record amount of books and book sales.

Now I'm returning to form and writing fiction. This volume is more production and editing-focused, as that was where I spent my time. I also believe this is a great way to start a new year that (at the time of this writing) still seems just as uncertain as 2020.

Sometimes the best thing to do is the only thing you can do: write.

My Core Strategic Priorities

. . .

As a refresher, my mission is to create content that entertains and/or educates my audience, preferably both, and to remain nimble in an ever-changing industry. I do this by focusing on five strategic priorities:

- Become a world-class content creator
- Become a world-class marketer
- Become a technology-driven writer
- Become a data-driven writer
- Become the writer of the future

I believe these five priorities are most important for me to have a long-term, sustainable career.

What's in This Volume

In this volume, I discuss a new challenge where I dictated while riding an exercise bike, and the incredible insights that came from it, including some weight loss!

In the World-Class Marketer section, I talk about some lessons I learned with advertising a poetry collection, Amazon keywords, and a big mistake I made with a book cover design this quarter that I hope won't hurt me too much.

I also talk about my return to dictation after several years, and new styles of dictating that have made me insanely more productive.

There is also a large section in this book about an editing data and analytics project. I've described my ideas for this project in previous volumes under the title of a "personal editing rules engine." This quarter, I finally deployed it, and the results are mind-blowing. I've cleared the way to producing squeaky-clean manuscripts free of grammar errors and typos. A good deal of the technology and data sections are dedicated to the editing project because it's a huge leap forward in my production process.

I also spend some time talking about new thoughts around my editing process, and how I've developed a more nuanced approach to research, self-editing, and working with my editors.

Additionally, I also give an update on items that I mentioned in the last volume, such as applying for a TED Talk and my 2021+ author strategy.

And, as always, I offer some fun ideas you can steal in your writing business. No volume of *Indie Author Confidential* would be complete without some bold ideas!

Enjoy, and happy 2021.

M.L. Ronn
Des Moines, Iowa
February 3, 2021

BECOME A WORLD-CLASS
CONTENT CREATOR

BE A GLACIER

You're either shrinking or expanding, so they say.

I was watching a video interview with Arnold Schwarzenegger, and the Governator was talking about his workout routine. Interestingly, it made me think of my *writing routine.*

What's the typical workout routine? Legs day, arms day, cardio day, rest.

What if your writing routine was "writing day," "self-improvement day," rinse and repeat? Or something else like "writing day," "marketing day," "business day," and so on?

You can get obnoxious with this, of course, but it's a great concept. I've always struggled with finding a balance between writing and marketing, and this is the simplest way I can think to fix it.

Write every day, but on the days when writing is not primary, meet your quota and then focus on something else.

I've been doing that the past few days as I write this chapter. Day A is a writing day. Day B is a self-improvement day. Self-improvement happens to include marketing.

When I'm writing, I'm shrinking. I'm pouring what I know onto the page, and my brain is smaller afterward.

When I'm learning, I'm expanding.
It's like a glacier.
Fun thought exercise.

LESSONS LEARNED FROM AN UNPRODUCTIVE WEEK

The second week of January 2021 was the most unproductive week I had in a long time. My entire writing business came to a screeching halt, even the manuscript I was working on.

A family member had some health issues that I needed to deal with.

My boss at work tendered her resignation. She'd hired me two months prior and my future was uncertain.

I had an urgent deadline I needed to hit for *Writer's Digest*, and I was contractually obligated to do so.

Rioters stormed the United States Capitol building, causing damage and threatening the fabric of American democracy.

I was already dealing with a rough spot in *Dead Rat Walking*. The events of the week stopped.

I had to walk away from everything and handle the issues in my personal life. I stopped writing, and the only writing-related items I did were continuing my podcast episodes and daily blogs. Aside from that, I did nothing.

That's unusual for me. I am tirelessly productive, even on bad days. I'm always looking for ways to move my writing efforts forward, and generally, I do. I don't take vacations from writing, and any time off is usually because of personal circumstances.

Unproductive weeks happen to the best of us, even prolific writers.

I dealt with it by walking away for a short amount of time until it was safe and productive to return to the desk.

It means that I had to push my finish date of *Dead Rat Walking* back by one week. It also meant that I put more stress on myself to hit my deadline. But overall, I'm glad I took the week off to recalibrate, focus my thoughts, and take care of myself and my family.

If I had continued writing during that period, I would have been so distracted that the words and progress I made in the business wouldn't have been worth it. In fact, I might have made *mistakes* that could have been costly and time-consuming to fix later.

In times like this, I remember the law of averages: if you (try to) write every day for 365 days, you're going to have an amazing word count at the end of the year, even if you miss a couple of weeks here and there. That's the case for me. The fact that I lost one week in January isn't going to stop me from publishing a lot of books this year.

This experience retaught me how important it is to stop and reflect every once in a while. I have a high-octane personality and am always thinking about what's next. Sometimes you just have to think about "what's now." The next always takes care of itself.

NAVIGATING A BUSY SEASON

My final semester of law school began this quarter. I'll be done in May 2021.

The start of the spring semester is always busy. It's when I hit my peak season and everything feels like it's on the verge of breaking apart if I'm not careful. What's on my plate:

1. Writing books
2. Marketing my books
3. Working a full-time job
4. Studying for classes
5. Raising a family
6. Working part-time for the Alliance of Independent Authors
7. Teaching insurance classes
8. Managing my emails
9. Producing content for my YouTube channel, daily blog, and three podcasts

Things get crazy around mid-terms. Somehow I always survive. I'm looking forward to eliminating law school from the equation forever, as I found that it added almost enough pressure to break everything.

But I persist. And this semester got me thinking about the processes I've followed to stay sane and on top of everything.

- I batch content ahead of time for my YouTube channel and podcasts. I try to preschedule as much content as I can, giving me as much breathing room as possible.
- I halt any major appointments or business decisions around mid-terms and finals.
- I rely greatly on the automation I've set up in all areas of my business. It pays off dividends, especially during a busy season like this.
- I let my audience know when things will get busy so they know if I am not as present, there is a reason. Communicating with my audience is key.
- I clear my inbox to zero at the beginning of the semester. It doesn't last me long, but it lasts me enough to get through the first two weeks or so.
- I work ahead in my class. I typically finish reading the textbook about a month before finishing the class. It's a painful investment, but I find that once I've finished reading the textbook, the amount of time I spend on the class drops dramatically, sometimes by 50 percent.
- I hire people more. I've hired part-time assistants to help me with one-off tasks that I don't have the time or energy to do. That helped me a lot, especially with video editing.

Anyway, life is hectic for me, but my goals are to keep momentum, to keep moving forward, and to be as consistent as possible. In just a few months, I'll have a lot more time per year, so I'll be able to breathe.

But I've found that learning how to anticipate and manage busy seasons is one of the secrets to my productivity. Where others would quit writing altogether, I maintain my writing and have benefited from it in a big way.

A LETTER TO MY 2014 WRITER SELF

I talk to writers all the time. Being a new writer isn't easy. It's a unique experience that I believe becomes harder to relate to the further away from you are from it.

There's so much to learn and the journey is an emotional rollercoaster. It's hard to think clearly, and even harder to make sound decisions because learning how to be a self-published writer is like drinking through a firehose. Every decision you make will have long-term consequences that you can't comprehend...and you can't think long-term because you're so focused on the *now* of creating the book. And on top of all that, there's the stress of money, time spent away from your family, and the nagging thought in the back of your head about whether all this time, money, and energy you're spending on a *dream* is going to work out.

Yet new writers are endlessly optimistic. It's a beautifully complicated, emotional, and optimistic time to be alive.

This got me thinking about what advice I would give to my 2014 self. If I could travel back in time to give writing advice to myself, what would I say?

. . .

Dear Michael,

Greetings from 2021! Though we are separated by seven years, I understand you very well because I am you.

Congratulations on writing your first book, How to Be Bad. It was an amazing feat to pull off, but you did it.

I regret to inform you that it won't sell very well, despite your optimism. In fact, you'll rebrand the book in a few years and it still won't sell.

But I have good news: as I write this letter, I've just started production on my fifty-fourth book, and it will probably sell pretty well!

It won't be until 2020 that you see the type of success you expect, and even then, you won't be making a living. But you'll be proud.

If I may, I'd like to give you some advice.

1. *Now that you've written your first book, you know the territory of a writer. It will never get easier to write a book, but you'll improve your confidence.*
2. *Keep reading voraciously and never stop. It will be difficult to balance writing, reading, business, and marketing, but it will be vital to find harmony between them.*
3. *You'll win (almost) every time you follow your instinct.*
4. *The more you write, the more you will succeed.*
5. *Learn how to use Amazon and Facebook ads without ignoring them at first, for God's sake!*

Keep doing what you're doing. There will be many nights where you'll question whether this will work out. There will be times when you feel like it won't work out, especially when you publish book after book and don't see the financial numbers you'd like to see.

But your experience is valuable and people all over the world will be watching you every day to see how you are doing and what you think about things related to the writing life.

Keep documenting your journey and keep finding ways to connect with your readers.

Sincerely,
   Future Michael

I don't think that letter scratches the surface of deep advice, and that brings me what I truly learned in this exercise: you can't skip past being new. No advice can truly help you. You're going to do what you're going to do, and if you're lucky, one day you'll wake up, realize that you've made enough mistakes, and start truly seeking advice that will be meaningful. You'll be frustrated at that point, but you'll find the advice that works best for you. This didn't happen for me until early 2015.

The key is that hopefully you haven't made career-ending mistakes, such as signing a bad contract, falling prey to a scam, or getting your publishing accounts canceled because you used bad judgment with a marketing technique. If you didn't do any of those things, you're golden. If you did, you may not have a career.

So if you're reading this and are a new author, just focus on surviving and try to avoid dumb mistakes that will end your career. Do that and you'll move to the next phase of your career, which is a lot calmer, less emotional, and (God willing) more productive and financially rewarding.

ALL THINGS IN LIFE ARE CYCLICAL

This is a long story, but I promise there is something good at the end (a couple of things, actually).

Growing up, I was a strange kid. I had an unusual taste in music. Even at a very young age, I was a jazz aficionado. My gateway to jazz (like a lot of people) was Steely Dan. Back when I was a kid, there were two types of people: those who had intense emotional experiences when they heard the music of Steely Dan for the first time, and those who thought Steely Dan was a joke. (Actually, that's still true today. If you're a Steely Dan fan, you understand me 100 percent. They still don't get the love they deserve.)

Since around the age of five or so, I was attracted to stuff in music that I couldn't explain, but I knew it when I heard it—mainly chords, harmony, composition, emotion. Other people just cared about lyrics, the groove, and whether they could relate to what the singer was singing about.

I wanted to be a musician for a long time. One day in high school (2002ish), I happened to share some of my music with my uncle, who was a band manager for a very popular local band in St. Louis that achieved international acclaim. He listened to my songs and brought up a crate of CDs that he had picked up while on tour. He thought I should check them out. To this day, I have no idea how my uncle compiled a crate of Japanese pop and funk CDs.

On the very top of the crate was the *Natsuko* album by Carlos Toshiki & Omega Tribe. I had never heard of them before, but I was used to listening to music in Japanese because I collected video game music. Plus, as someone who listened to jazz, I was used to international artists.

I inspected the album, and to my surprise, on the back cover was a black man sitting on a couch with some Japanese guys. I was intrigued...a black man, a member of a Japanese band???

To say the album blew me away was an understatement. The Omega Tribe to this day remains one of my favorite bands of all time. I own all their work. Their music helped me get through a rough freshman year in high school.

I was fascinated by the fact that a black man sang with them, wrote songs, and performed as a full member of the band, and not merely a backup singer.

I didn't know this at the time, but the band was part of a gigantic musical movement in Japan called "city pop," which, in a nutshell, is 80s pop infused with jazz chords, with very high composition and production value. I won't get into city pop here —look it up sometime.

Anyway, I was hooked on city pop in 2002 before ANYONE in the states (that I know of personally) knew what it was. Everyone I knew thought I was crazy importing records from Japan. They didn't see the point of listening to music you couldn't understand. But for me, it was about more than that.

I always respected Joey McCoy for his story and his contribution to the musical genre, even though I didn't know much about him. I credit him and the Omega Tribe with my gateway into a genre that I have become a lifelong fan of.

In 2017, I wrote a novel called *Honor's Reserve* and even named the lead character of the series after McCoy (Grayson McCoy). I shared a similar story of how I discovered him in an author's note at the back of the book.

(I named every lead character in my *Galaxy Mavericks* series after my favorite musicians. It was fun, but until today, I didn't think anything would come of it).

Fast forward to 2021, and some very interesting things have happened.

First, city pop is mainstream now. Awareness of the genre started in the early 2010s with the Vaporwave movement. Vaporwave is an underground music movement where artists take old recordings from the 80s and 90s, slow them down, chop them up, and add effects such as distortion to create a completely new experience. While the genre itself is controversial because of copyright infringement issues, it made the 80s and 90s cool again because it made millennials like myself reminisce about our childhoods. It's also a way to discover new music because listeners like to seek out the original tracks that inspired the Vaporwave versions. Vaporwave is the millennial reincarnation of crate diving at a record store. When artists started using city pop songs as the basis for Vaporwave tracks, many people discovered the genre. That's one way that city pop became mainstream.

There were also viral videos. The song that pretty much blew the Internet open was "Plastic Love" by Mariya Takeuchi. It has 48 million views and counting at the time of this writing. I knew this song before it was cool.

Suddenly, English speakers discovered what I had fallen in love with almost 20 years ago. Now, city pop is cool, but trust me, it wasn't like that in 2002 or even 2008. The only way you could get it (if you even knew about it) was to import records or find it in other clandestine ways. One of those ways was buying digital iTunes Japan gift cards, switching over to the Japanese version of the iTunes Store, and then searching for your favorite artists in kanji, but only then you got 30-second samples, so it was hard to find good songs. But you could buy stuff there before Apple locked down their international stores. I told you I was serious about this stuff...

Anyway, city pop is having a moment. (Somewhat) Mainstream artists like Thundercat and Benny Sings have paid tribute to it. This past year, Apple Music and Spotify onboarded a CRAPTON of city pop music—something that you would have never been able to find just a year or two ago. It's still very weird to play city pop on Apple Music.

All those artists who found success in Japan but almost nowhere else are now having their moment, with a generation of young people who were either barely alive or nonexistent when the music was recorded. Record companies are finally figuring it out and cashing in on it (in a good way).

When I found a bunch of city pop albums on Apple Music, I was surprised to see that there was some more information on the bands available in English on the Internet. On a random whim, I discovered that someone had created a Wikipedia page for Joey McCoy, which was neat to see.

And to my shock, I saw MY NAME on the Wikipedia page. Someone referenced my author's note in the back of *Honor's Reserve* and posted on the page that I had named one of my characters after him.

Ironically, Google Books indexed *Honor's Reserve* and just happened to include the page from my author's note where I talked about Joey McCoy. That was how the person discovered the reference. How random is that?

It turns out that Joey McCoy even recorded an album of his own that long-time Omega Tribe fans are just now discovering and buzzing about on Reddit and other places.

(I'm fairly certain that I sold a few copies of *Honor's Reserve* from that Wikipedia page—it rarely sells any copies these days, but I've noticed sales starting up again—nothing substantial, but noticeable. I don't actively advertise it.

There are a lot of people right now giving Joey his props. It seems he's moved on from his music career, but how amazing is it that he's still alive to see people from all corners of the world appreciating his musical skills. Not every artist gets that honor. It's too bad that he's probably not getting compensated that much for the recognition.

All right, so what does this have to do with you?

Everything is cyclical.

So what you published a book that gets zero sales? What if something happens in the cultural zeitgeist 30 years from now that makes younger generations interested in your work?

Sure, it's a long time, but you never know, right?

And, what if, instead of quitting, that you were still writing 30 years from now (if you're still alive), and you have a crapton of books that new generations can discover?

That, my friends, is what this post is about.

Everything has its time. If an obscure 80s genre from Japan can catch on fire worldwide, then maybe one of your books can too.

That's why you shouldn't give up. This isn't the 80s, where it was hard to maintain a career if the planets didn't align. Now you can have a career forever and continue to get paid for your work. You just have to have the courage to write, publish, and keep your book for sale. And it can earn money for you long after you publish it.

This is the greatest time in the history of the world to be a writer.

WRITING AN ARTICLE FOR WRITER'S DIGEST

I received an opportunity to write for *Writer's Digest* magazine, which was an amazing honor. The opportunity came because the editor happened to watch a video I produced back in 2014.

Ironically, I almost didn't record this *exact video*. I had to change the lighting in my basement because I filmed my old videos down there. The lighting, which was pretty good in my early videos, was never the same. I hated it.

This particular video was one of the first videos I recorded in the new lighting, and as much as I hated it, I published it anyway because I didn't want to miss a week of producing content. The video garners few views, and I never thought twice about it.

Fast forward to 2021 when my video setup is much better, more sophisticated, and the content is better...and the video that prompted her to reach out was the 2014 one. If that's not evidence that you should create content even though it's not your best, I don't know what is.

Anyway, we discussed writing an article about writer's block.

I read several back issues of the magazine and got a feel for what current contributors were writing. I also searched what people were saying about the magazine. I got a sense of what to write and how to say it. The magazine's target audience is newer writers, so I needed to speak to them at a higher level but still deliver deep value, and in a way they've never heard before. Then, I had to tie that to the magazine's vision and aesthetics, *and* meet their word count quota.

Somehow the balancing act worked, and I wrote an article called: *Drift: The Curiously Effective Way to Beat Procrastination.* It will debut in the May/June 2021 edition of the magazine.

THE WRITING WHILE MOVING CHALLENGE

In the last volume of this series, I discussed a wild and wacky idea for a project that involved an exercise bike, a novel, and a lot of ingenuity. I called it "the writing while moving challenge."

I have an exercise bike that is getting lonely. I need to write new fiction. I am also fat and need to lose weight. Why not address all three problems at the same time?

I also need to write more books under my urban fantasy pen name.

Here's the idea: I will exercise for at least 60 minutes every day. While exercising, I will dictate a new novel. I can only write via dictation, I can only dictate while I am on the bike, and I cannot use my hands, except to correct outrageous errors by my dictation software, Dragon. I speak an average of 150 to 160 words per minute. That is approximately 9,000 words per day and 63,000 words per week. Theoretically, that would net me 270,000 words per year, which is approximately 5.4 novels at 50,000 words each.

But it gets better. Dictation is quite infamous for its accuracy issues. Even a top-of-the-line program like Dragon can make a lot of mistakes while you dictate. In many ways, you must learn to speak and think differently as you are telling your story. Many find this method of writing difficult; I find it intriguing.

In 2016, I dictated my *The Last Dragon Lord* series in Dragon. I also wrote that series into the dark, which means that I did not outline the story; I just wrote whatever came into my head, and then fixed it as I went. I also wrote the series in one draft. This is extraordinarily difficult to do with dictation, but I managed it.

It's such an interesting concept. What if, on this exercise bike, I wrote an entire series via dictation into the dark AND in one draft? That's a little crazy... But I'm willing to do it because I need to write new fiction, and I am full of new ideas that I want to get on to paper.

So I started the challenge around the middle of December 2020, not knowing where it would go. In fact, I practiced for the challenge by dictating this very chapter that you're reading! This chapter was my first official test to see how it went.

My first challenge at the time of this writing is to figure out which story I want to write, do the basic research, figure out what the first scene is, and then write it.

I also want to know how much a novel is worth in pounds and miles. Generally, it takes me approximately 40 hours to write and prepare one of my novels for publication. What would that look like in pounds and miles? I am fascinated to know the answer.

2021 is a new year and I want to get healthier as a writer. I believe that this is the ultimate test of writing skill and complexity.

Anyway, it's time for me to get off the bike now, so I'm going to stop. I look forward to dictating more chapters and letting you know how this goes!

. . .

My Setup

Here's what the dictation setup looks like. I attached a microphone boom arm to the desk and put my Blue Yeti Microphone on it. Then I used an old text book to prop up my computer.

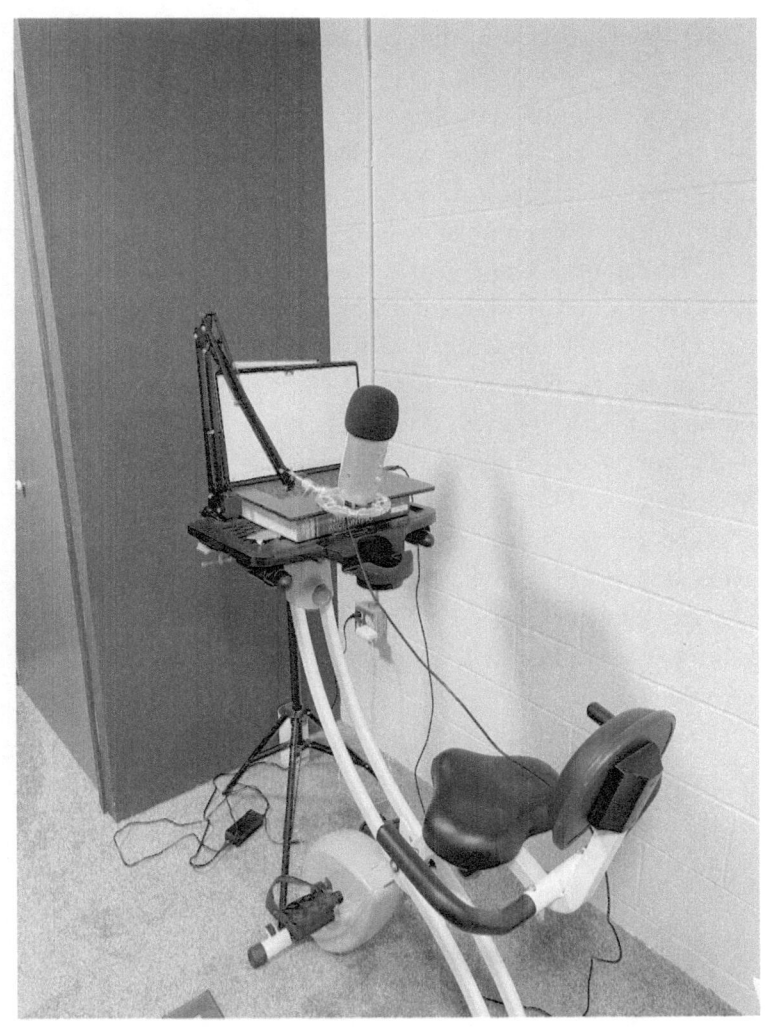

How It Went

. . .

Okay, I'm not dictating this section. But this project was a success.

I started off only dictating on the bike, but my first few days were so high word-count wise that I decided to incorporate other ways of writing into the project, such as writing on my laptop and writing on my phone.

The results: I wrote 60,000 words in 30 days. I had a bad week where I didn't write any words at all, so if you take that out, I technically wrote the novel in 21 days.

I used the bike 50 percent of the days that I wrote and burned 1,050 calories and traveled 31.5 miles in approximately 630 minutes (10.5 hours). The challenge also netted me around five pounds lost!

The entire project probably took around 30 hours, so I spent at least a third of that moving, which is great.

Speed-wise, this is not my fastest novel. My fastest record is seven days. My longest is 18 months. But this novel does rank near the top.

Lessons I learned:

- It's easy to tell your story while moving; it just requires a mindset shift.
- Writing into the dark and in one draft is indeed possible on an exercise bike.
- Whenever I didn't know what to write next, hopping on the bike helped me with the writer's block. I thought being on the bike would have the opposite effect.
- The sections I wrote on the bike were nearly indistinguishable from the sections I wrote by hand or on my phone (to me, at least).
- I noticed considerably better sleep and general well-being throughout the project and afterward.

- My highest word count day was well over 5,000 words of clean fiction with no cleanup required. For me, a usual fiction writing day (typing) is somewhere between 1,000 and 2,000 words.
- There were some days where I wouldn't have been able to write at all, but a 30-minute dictation session at night netted me a word count that looked as if I didn't struggle at all that day.
- Because this book required a fair amount of research on subject matter that I wasn't familiar with, I had to stop frequently to research.
- When I wasn't writing at my computer, I wrote the book on my phone and also dictated on my phone while doing tasks such as laundry and dishes.
- I also dictated the novel while walking around my office, untethered to my keyboard and computer.

Overall, this novel was many different writing styles all converging into the final product. I have some more thoughts on this in the Writer of the Future section, but the willingness to experiment with a new way of writing paid off, and it made me more flexible with my storytelling in the future.

IMPROVING MY RESEARCH PROCESS WITH FACT-CHECKERS

I recently finished my 30th novel. It's crazy to think that I have written so many novels since 2013, but this was a great opportunity for me to reevaluate how I produce my books, and how I can produce them more efficiently in the future.

I believe that every few dozen novels or so, it's a good idea to test your processes and your assumptions to see where your weaknesses are. I have written enough novels at this point to have production down to a science, but I still feel that there are areas where I could do better.

One of those areas is in research. Research is a major time suck for a writer. The hardest part is knowing what to research, where to find it, and what to use. I know a lot of writers who spend hours if not months researching elements for their novel, only to not use most of it. That is woefully inefficient.

I wrote a book called *How to Write Your First Novel*, and it is one of my better-selling books for writers. In it, I talk about breaking up research into two categories: foundational research and just-in-time research.

Foundational research is research that you need to do to start writing. Nothing more, nothing less. For example, if your book takes place in the city of Chicago, and you don't live in Chicago, you need to do a lot of research to portray the Chicago parts properly on the page. In this way, foundational research helps you create the foundation for your story.

All research *after* you start writing is just-in-time research. You research what you need when you need it. Instead of spending hours or months researching a topic, simply write the story. Then, when you come to a section that you're not sure about, stop writing and go research. In my opinion, this is far more efficient than frontloading your research because you are only researching what you need. Everything you find with just-in-time research ends up in the novel. Unless you write in a genre that requires in-depth research such as regency romance or historical fiction, this is a far better way to tackle the problem of research.

I have used foundational research and just-in-time research for years, and this technique has helped make my novels more realistic and accurate. However, how good is my research? In other words, how do I know if the details that I am researching are accurate?

I have been experimenting with fact-checking my research in recent novels. It's one thing to research subject matter in your book, but another thing entirely to verify that your research is accurate.

I find that every novel I write has about two or three subject matter areas that I need help in. My most recent novel took place in the city that I don't live in, featured an animal that I was not familiar with, and featured a sibling relationship, which was new territory for me. I did as much research as I could, but I had this nagging feeling that I needed to have someone look at the novel to verify if what I wrote made sense.

This is where the concept of fact-checking comes in. You recruit several people to evaluate what you have written to verify if you executed properly on your research. You can research a topic until you know it inside out, but there's a difference between knowing something well and writing it accurately. Fact-checkers test your skill as a writer.

With my newest novel, I recruited three different groups of fact-checkers: one group who live or had lived in the city of Chicago for a very long time and were familiar with it; another group who were familiar with rodent biology, and who had degrees in biology or bioengineering; and a final group who were female fantasy readers who had younger brothers and who had given them relationship advice (something that happens in the novel with my main character and his sister).

I explained to the fact-checkers what I was looking for, and I gave them basic instructions. Then I sent them excerpts from the novel that contained items that needed to be fact-checked. For example, I sent my Chicago fact-checkers only the sections about Chicago, my biology fact-checkers only the sections about biology, and my female readers only the chapters from the point of view of the hero's sister (who featured prominently in the story). It was a little awkward sending them only parts of the novel, but I believe this was more respectful of their time. It also allowed them to get through comments much faster. Most of the fact-checkers took less than a week to provide their feedback.

The result? We'll see. I believe that, ultimately, readers decide the merits of the story, but I want to do all I can to make sure that they have an enjoyable reading experience and that little technical details don't pull them out of the story. In fact, if I can get these technical details right, it will enhance readers' enjoyment of the story.

This technique was inspired by mega-bestseller Arthur Hailey, who was a household name in the 1960s and 1970s. Many of his novels topped the *New York Times* bestseller list.

I am a big fan of Arthur Hailey and consider him to be one

of my all-time favorites. I was pleasantly surprised when I discovered that his wife, Sheila, wrote a biography of how she met him and their marriage. The biography talked about Arthur's writing process and how he researched his novels. His novels take place in a single setting such as an airport, hotel, bank, or auto factory, and it features thriller plots from the perspective of the employees who work there. When you read his novels, you get the sense that he has meticulously researched every element of the places where he sets his novels. Fortunately, Sheila talked about his process in the book. She mentioned how he took copious notes, read as many books as he could about the topics he needed to research, and even conducted field interviews with industry experts (I imagine that being a *New York Times* bestseller will open a lot of doors with industry executives). For his book *Wheels,* he worked on an assembly line for a few hours to understand line workers. He would take pages and pages of notes, organize them using a notecard system, and then incorporate his research into his novels as he wrote.

Reading about his thought process got me thinking about my research process. I write science fiction and fantasy, so the level of research I need is not as substantial as Arthur Hailey's, but good research is a bedrock of good fiction.

The feedback my fact-checkers gave me was amazing. Not only did they answer the questions that I posed to them with good detail, but they also described how they think about certain issues, which was more helpful than the actual feedback they provided. I found that learning how someone thinks about something and why they think the way they do is an underrated window into writing more engaging characters. For example, my Chicago fact-checkers had very strong opinions about certain things in the city, such as gentrification.

When you can get inside people's heads, you can exercise

mind control on the page because you can go deeper into an issue or explore different perspectives of an issue that readers haven't considered, lending more authenticity to the novel. That's gold for a fiction writer.

To find my fact-checkers, I used my network and asked for help on my podcasts and daily blog. Several of my readers reached out offering help, which was humbling. I also found fact-checkers on Upwork.com. I posted a job with a description of what I needed with a small budget and a one-week turn-around, and I screened applicants based on their experience and responses to interview questions in the job description. My Chicago fact-checking job attracted almost 70 people who lived in the city or were very familiar with the city. In short, it's not hard to find people who have the experience you need. You just need to ask for it.

Another area where you can weave fact-checking into your book is through beta reading. I believe the beta readers ' life experience is an underrated resource that writers don't tap in to. For example, beta readers are not just readers; they are parents, professionals in an industry, members of their community, and so on. They have hobbies other than reading and unique perspectives on life that they are willing to share if you ask them. When you lead by asking for these types of experiences, you can attract higher quality people to help you with your story. Let's say that you have a fantasy novel that has religious overtones based on Judaism. Why not look for a fantasy reader who is a devout follower of the Jewish religion and deeply involved in their synagogue and the Jewish community as one of your *beta readers*? Most people don't think about that; they just want to find anyone and everyone willing to beta read for them, missing out on their life experiences.

In my opinion, it is better to have beta readers with the experience you're looking for than generic beta readers who will read anything. I no longer recruit beta readers who don't exclusively read in the genre I write in, for example. A reader who is well-versed in the genre always gives better feedback than someone who "just likes to read everything."

I enjoyed the fact-checking process so much that I have decided to make it a part of all of my novels moving forward. I believe it made a measurable difference in the quality of the novel.

SOME THOUGHTS ON EDITORS

Few lessons I have learned are more important than those I have learned while working with an editor.

Editing is subjective. You don't know whether you hired a good editor until after you publish your book. This is because readers are the ultimate arbiters of quality, not the writer or editor.

Your book can be squeaky clean and free of typos, but readers still might not buy it if there are issues with the story.

Just because YOU feel good about your story, that doesn't mean your readers will like it. You can hire a developmental editor, copy editor, proofreader, and even utilize beta readers and sensitivity readers, but readers may still dislike your story. Yet the common wisdom is to hire as many editors as you can afford and hope that it makes a difference.

In recent years, I have taken a more nuanced approach to editing.

Most people think of editing in three phases: developmental, copyediting, proofreading. I don't personally believe in developmental editing, but it is a valid method. Copyediting, however, has two distinct phases. Understanding these two phases will help you write better stories. The first phase of copy-editing is what I call continuity editing. This is not developmental editing; rather, it is about the continuity and cohesion of your story. A developmental editor will look at your story and recommend structural changes if the editor feels it is needed. My vision of a continuity editor does not recommend structural changes; in fact, those are out of the question unless there is a serious plot hole. Instead, they focus on making sure that the content *within* your existing structure is cohesive, typically at the sentence and chapter level. All line edits they recommend are a direct consequence of inconsistencies they find. So this type of editor *needs* to be a skilled copyeditor.

Here are some examples of "continuity editing."

First example: your character's eyes are blue on page 2, but green on page 10. This is a classic continuity issue that an editor can help you with.

Second example: your character's actions don't make logical sense to the reader. For example, if your character is carrying four grocery bags to their car, and they just open the car door and get in, a reader might say "Wait a minute...If the character is caring that many bags, shouldn't they put one of the bags down and open the door?" Then, the reader might put your book down. A good continuity editor can help you avoid this problem.

The third example: plot holes. Let's say that your character has a sword that gets destroyed in chapter 30, but then the sword magically reappears in chapter 40 with no explanation. This is also a continuity problem.

These are precisely the type of errors you want to eliminate because they pull readers out of the story. A continuity editor looks at your story in both the macro and micro to help you root out these issues.

However, many authors don't often think about their story

in terms of internal continuity. They just send it to a copyeditor and hope that the editor will catch both continuity *and* grammatical errors.

In my experience of writing over 30 novels, very few editors I've worked with specialize in catching both continuity and grammar errors consistently. While they *will* certainly catch both, they're usually good at catching one or the other. I've worked with over a dozen editors, and when you work with that many people, you notice things.

I discovered this nuance by accident. I was interviewing for copyeditors and requested sample edits of the first chapter from the two top candidates. What happened next completely changed how I see copyediting.

The first editor was an ace at catching continuity issues—this person caught things in the first chapter alone that most editors would have missed. Just thinking about their edits even now, I shake my head at the little micro-detail she found, combined throughout the novel. There was no way I *couldn't* hire this person. However, they missed a LOT of line editing issues, more than I was comfortable with. That said, they gave me a great edit. There's value in having someone with their type of mind.

The second editor gave me a solid line edit that was as good as any I've ever received, but they missed many of the continuity issues that the first editor caught. There was no way I couldn't hire this person, either.

If I hired one editor, I would have grammar issues, and if I hired the other, I would have continuity issues. When you put both editors' work products together, you got a full, comprehensive edit.

That got me thinking about my prior editors. I reviewed their work and discovered that while they were good in both categories, each editor demonstrated an above-average skill level one category over the other. It was uncanny.

That experience taught me to start screening editors in terms of their strengths, and that while there are editors who excel in both categories, it's more realistic to hire two people to help you with continuity, spelling, and grammar. It also provides you with diversity of thought, which is never a bad thing.

THE BOOK COVER DESIGN PARADOX AND THE LOOMING DESIGNER SHORTAGE

I needed a cover designer recently, and I discovered that the market changed substantially since the last time I ordered a fiction cover design in 2019.

I visited the websites of all the designers that I'd used in the past. All of them had either raised their rates between 20-50 percent or were no longer accepting commissions. That was a bummer.

Then I researched new cover designers and had a hard time finding a designer whose aesthetic jibed with my tastes. Those I *did* find had waiting lists of six months or more!

(Waiting periods have always been a problem with designers. As they take on more clients, the waiting period goes up and you have to be strategic about getting on their calendar. But still...)

I'm not indicting designers. They're just running their businesses. But I'm running a business too...

As someone who produces novels quickly, I can't tolerate a six-month or more waiting period.

Don't we always talk about writing and publishing fast in our community? Isn't the common advice to publish often? How can you do that with six-month or more waiting periods? It makes planning a lot more difficult. I find that to be an interesting contradiction.

So what's a writer to do?

I did more research, and found that the cost of cover design in general had gone up substantially in just two years.

Earlier than 2019, you could find a pre-made cover for less than $75. At the time of this writing, you would be lucky if you could find a decent premade cover for under $200.

Earlier than 2019, you could find a decent cover designer for between $300 and $500. Now you would be lucky if you found a decent cover designer for under $400. The most expensive designers used to be around $600-$700; now I see high-end cover designers charging well over $700 – *and* with a six-month or more waiting period!

This sounded alarm bells for me.

The costs of cover design are increasing, but you're not getting any more for your money than you got two years ago. I attribute this to the fact that designers have to pay their bills, and they're getting pickier about their clients. I also blame the pandemic.

If this trend continues, we're headed for a cover designer shortage. There won't be enough people to fill the demand. Therefore, the prices and waiting periods for good designers will keep going up.

For someone as prolific as me who publishes around 7 to 10 books per year, most of them based on my whims, that's a problem because I can't plan ahead! It's hard to have publishing flexibility when you have to wait longer than two or three months. Ideally, you want as few waiting periods as possible.

Also, it's worth pointing out that if we're seeing the costs increase today, what will they be two years from now? Ten years? You're going to pay more, wait longer, have to switch designers frequently, and you'll get nothing more for your money.

This is most disastrous for new writers. If the trends continue, there could be a day when a new writer has to pay $1,000 or more just to get an average cover.

A full-time writer and bestseller is less likely to care about this problem because they can afford the extra few hundred dollars. They may make well over that (in profits) in a single day. So while they may not like it, they'll chalk it up to the cost of doing business.

The ones who get squeezed are the authors in the beginning and middle of their journeys...authors who are working full-time jobs, with families, who don't have unlimited money, and who are (rightly so) worried about the financial prospects of "making it" as a writer. What about them?

This problem does not exist with editors. Editors raise their rates and leave the industry all the time, but you can always find someone else.

You can always find an editor to suit your budget. If I wanted, I could attract an editor in twenty-four hours and have them working on my book by the end of the week. Prices are going up somewhat, probably tracking with the costs of living, but they're far more manageable on the editing side. This problem is unique to cover design.

I haven't heard anyone else talking about this problem, so for now, I'm talking to myself, but there are three solutions to this problem that I can think of.

The first is to learn how to design your own book covers. If you can do that, you'll save money and avoid waiting periods. In fact, it's the greatest cost-saving and production efficiency I can think of as a writer. You would cut your production costs by *at least* half, making it far more affordable to publish flexibly, and rapidly.

You can learn to create a decent book cover with enough time, energy, and money. There are online courses you can take. If you read prior volumes of *Indie Author Confidential*, you'll know that I have written that there is a demand for more detailed instruction of this kind. An influencer designer who wanted to build a big following could do so by teaching authors how to create their own book covers step-by-step, in a professional way that gets results.

However, most writers I know of don't have an appetite for creating their own covers, nor do they have the skill level to do it. Also, anything you create as a writer is likely to be inferior to what a professional cover designer can create for you, no matter how much time, money, and effort you put into learning how to do it yourself. There are downsides. But in the future, if you want a cover quickly, you may not have another choice.

For my novel, I was lucky enough to find someone with only a two-month waiting period with only a slightly increased cost. I might not be so lucky next time, so I'm planning for that now.

I hope I'm wrong, but if I'm not, a crisis awaits. In the coming years, I don't foresee that the number of new (good) designers entering the market will outpace the existing (good) ones who have higher costs, longer wait times, or a full client list.

It makes good sense to start learning how to do your own covers now. Hire a designer to create a cover template that features your name prominently. Then just use that template as the basis for the covers you create yourself.

The second solution to this problem is technology. Perhaps in the future, there will be artificial intelligence that uses computer vision to help you design covers that are more high-quality than what you can do on your own. But even if it were possible, technology always has limitations and trade-offs and it won't save us completely.

The third solution is to hire your own cover designer to keep in-house or to enter into a contract with a designer that guarantees a certain amount of books for them each year in exchange for a fast turnaround time so you can "skip the line." Some designers may start offering this. For example, pay X amount and you'll get the cover in nine months. Or, pay Y amount and you'll get the cover in one month with more responsive service. Or, pay me Z amount and you'll get a discount and a better waiting period in exchange for a guaranteed amount of books. I don't like any of those options, frankly, because it creates more division between haves and have-nots, and it locks down designers from the general public. But if enough people complain about a shortage and waiting periods, I don't see how this doesn't become a reality.

In the future (read: today), the best-selling authors will lock down the talented cover designers, and it will be next to impossible to work with them. That's why we lowly writers have to start planning for an even worse iteration of this future. And that planning begins now.

If you have a good cover designer currently, write like hell and do everything in your power to keep them. Otherwise, when you find yourself in need of a new designer—and you will eventually, because it's only a matter of time before situations change—be prepared to pay more for the same product.

This is also an opportunity for alternative cover designer business models to arise, such as a business that operates with a team of designers instead of a solo operation. The companies that will win in the future with mid-list and new authors will be those who can create a cover in two months or less, rain or shine. Reliability of delivery is the future with cover designers. We don't have that now.

ROYAL ORDER OF EDITING

I've been thinking about something that I call "the royal order of editing." If one were to follow this, they would cover all of their bases.

Phase 1: Self-editing.

Phase 2: Alpha reader. An alpha reader is a first reader who reads the story and gives you feedback on whether it works.

Phase 3: Developmental editor.

Phase 4: Fact-checkers.

Phase 5: Continuity editing.

Phase 6: Beta readers.

Phase 7: Copyeditor.

Phase 8: Proofreader.

Phase 9: Advanced spelling and grammar checkers like Grammarly or ProWritingAid.

Is this "order" overkill? Probably. But it's helpful to think about with every project because some books need more editing than others.

TRYING TO GET MY MESSAGING RIGHT

When I was working on my sales database project, I struggled with how to explain it. At first, I was way too technical. Then I went in the opposite direction and was too high-level. Ultimately, it took two to three months for me to settle on the right message.

Later in this book, I'm going to discuss an editing data and analytics project I'm working on, and it poses the same risk:

- it will help authors be more efficient and productive with their self-editing;
- it's a highly technical project in nature, but the result is not; and
- it uses tools most authors have never heard of, or aren't familiar with.

This book is me documenting my journey, so I give myself permission to be a bit more detailed than normal. That's one of the main selling points of the *Indie Author Confidential* series. However, when I'm explaining the project on my podcast or

YouTube channel, or in passing to another influencer, I have to tell the right story, or people won't get it.

So that's where I am with this project right now. As you read the editing data and analytics chapters in the Data-Driven Writer section, I hope that I will explain the issue in language that helps you understand the project and the value it provides. If not, I'll keep trying.

BECOME A WORLD-CLASS MARKETER

NO HASSLE, NO BS MARKETING

I participated in a marketing promotion that included a bundle of writing books, courses, and more. One of my books was included. The bundle was a great product.

When customers bought the bundle, they could download my book by clicking a Book Funnel link.

A reader reached out after buying the bundle to thank me for not making it overly difficult to access my book. According to the reader, every other content creator in the bundle required customers to set up logins or give their email address to receive the creator's content.

I appreciated the note. I believe in making it easy to grab a product once you've purchased it. Sure, I could have used the opportunity to build an email list, but I chose not to.

I prefer that people download the book as easily and quickly as possible, and then if they like it, they can engage with me further.

This is the opposite of what most marketers would do. It's not a "marketing best practice" and I lose out on email subscribers in the short term, but I win in the long term because the people who *do* engage are more likely to consume my content and buy my books...mainly because I didn't spam them to death or chase after their engagement.

It's like dating. Go out with someone and see where it goes. Would *you* appreciate it if the person you're dating wants to get into your pants on the first date? Exactly.

Marketing is like that too.

BOOK SIRENS

A fellow writer sent me an email recommending that I check out a service called Book Sirens.

I did some research on the company, and I was pleasantly surprised. Book Sirens is a service that helps you secure book reviews from avid readers. It solves a (not so) age-old problem that self-published writers have had since the beginning of self-publishing as we know it: getting reviews.

When you publish your first book, you don't have an audience. So it's hard to go find people who would be willing to read your book in exchange for a review. A lot of people use Goodreads, reader forums, and other ways to reach prospective readers, but this comes with a risk. Book Sirens aims to eliminate this risk.

Here's how it works: the website is a community of avid readers who sign up for accounts in exchange for communications from the website. Authors upload their books to the site, and Book Sirens notifies readers that your book is available. Readers can then choose whether to download your book or not based on your cover and your description. You only pay when readers download your book. Of course, they don't have to leave a review, and some of them will not. However, Book Sirens states that many of their readers DO leave reviews. The great thing about this is that it doesn't violate Amazon's terms of service and it is an easy way to get your book into the hands of strangers.

Book Sirens isn't just for new writers, though. Even writers like me can take advantage of the service, leveraging it for new releases.

I've seen a lot of services come and go in the self-publishing community, but I've never seen anything quite like this. The website has amassed a very large community of eager readers, I've heard nothing but good things about it, AND it plays nice with the Amazon terms of service! I can't tell you how many times I have seen service providers in this community who violate Amazon's terms of service for one reason or another. I remember (not so fondly) a particular service that I used back in 2014 that promised to get you at least 50 to 100 reviews on your book by paying the service a finder's fee. Amazon decided one day that it didn't like this and they made it a personal mission to remove all reviews from its site from this service. The service did NOT violate Amazon's terms, but Amazon felt it was bad for customer trust.

I even remember a service that scraped Amazon's publicly available reviewer information for email addresses based on comparable books to yours, and then they provided you with a list of those reviewers' email addresses. That was pretty cool because you could email people with a cold pitch and get a pretty good response rate. But again, when Amazon found out about this service, they simply stopped making reviewer data discoverable to scraping software. There went yet another method of obtaining reviews. After that, I didn't think that there would be a legitimate way to procure reviews. And then I found

Book Sirens. I can't for the life of me find any way that their service violates any terms.

Also, the Alliance of Independent Authors has rated Book Sirens as "Recommended," which means that they give it a seal of approval, which is a pretty big deal given that the Alliance of Independent Authors is a watchdog organization that gives brutally honest reviews of self-publishing service providers.

I signed up for an account immediately. I haven't been able to use it because I don't have a new book to launch yet, but I plan to incorporate Book Sirens into my marketing strategy.

TO BOX SET OR NOT TO BOX SET?

In December 2020, I published volume 3 of my *Indie Author Confidential* series. I also used this opportunity to create an anthology collection that compiled volumes 1 through 3. I priced this at $9.99, which is a discount compared to buying all three volumes individually.

I've always struggled with this particular arrangement. Which book do you advertise? Do you send people to volume 1, or do you send people to the anthology?

Readers fall into both camps. Some people don't like to buy box sets for one reason or another; others prefer to have all books in one place if possible to keep their library cleaner.

This also becomes more complicated when you introduce Amazon Ads into the mix.

In the past, I haven't done a very good job of letting people know that an anthology exists. This time, I wanted to change that.

On the individual volumes 1 through 3, I updated the first line of the book description to let readers know that an anthology exists, and I included a link to where they can buy it.

I only advertised the anthology. I figured that advertising volume 1 individually would confuse things.

While it is too soon to determine whether this method worked, I am fine with it because it is the right thing to do for my readers. I also think it's fairer. No one likes to buy an individual book only to find out that they could have saved a few dollars by buying the anthology. Book retailers haven't exactly made it easy to discover anthologies either. In a perfect world, authors would be able to select a box that tells book retailers that a book exists in an anthology, and after the reader clicks the buy button, they would get a pop-up notifying them that the book they wish to buy also exists in a collection. If they wanted, they could click through to the collection or buy the book as they originally intended. In my opinion, that's the only way to solve this problem, and no retailer that I know of has this functionality.

Sure, I'll miss out on a couple of bucks from those people who choose to buy the anthology over the individual volumes, but the people who purchase individual volumes can also continue to do so if they please. Depending on how this goes, I may go back to some of my earlier box sets with fiction and try the same strategy.

IMPROVING THE AD CONVERSION RATE OF A POETRY COLLECTION

I have been scaling up my Amazon Ads. Until now, I only ran ads on my more popular books.

I expanded my ad campaigns to titles that historically haven't sold well, including my poetry collections, *Android Poems* and *Muse Poems*.

To my surprise, I was able to sell a handful of copies per month of each. My ad campaigns in general were more effective on my poetry collections than some of my fiction series!

Some of the techniques I used:

- I waited for 100 clicks before taking any action. This gives me enough of a sample size to decide on. When I ran the initial campaigns, there was very little interest in the collections. I receive clicks, but no sales. My conversion rate was around 1:35, which means that I only received a sale for every 35 clicks. For your ads to be profitable, you need around a 1:10 conversion rate. I lost a lot of money in the first 100 clicks.

- After 100 clicks, I rewrote the book description to make it read like newer, bestselling poetry collections that were similar to mine. The biggest change was to include a sample poem in the description. 100 clicks later, I improved my conversion ratio for *Android Poems* to 1:24 and I lost half as much money as I lost during the first 100 clicks. Major improvement, but not good enough. I made additional adjustments to the book description that brought me down to around 1:12, which is very profitable because most of the sales are for the paperback edition.
- *Muse Poems*, however, went in the opposite direction all the way down to 1:86. I believe it was because the sample poem wasn't resonating with readers. I switched it and brought my conversion rate back to around 1:24, which is where it is currently. I lose money on this collection every month, but I'm still selling copies and reaching readers, so that's worth the investment.

I'm blown away that I was able to get restore sales for my poetry collections. It just doesn't seem real. But *Android Poems* now turns me a tidy little profit every month and hopefully will long into the future.

CLUBHOUSE

One of my YouTube subscribers invited me to join Clubhouse, which is an invite-only social media network that is the "new kid on the block" at the time of this writing.

Clubhouse is an audio app that uses "rooms" where people gather to talk about topics that interest them. You can find rooms for writing, music, entrepreneurship, and much more (even rooms where people have contests to see who has the most sexual moans...not kidding).

Anyway, I tried Clubhouse and it was interesting, to say the least. It reminds me a lot of Anchor.FM. Most people know Anchor as a podcasting service, but it wasn't always that way. It was an audio app where people had their own "stations" and spoke whatever was on their mind in the form of short audiograms. You could reply to people's audiograms and start conversations, and listen in on other people's conversations. I liked the old version of Anchor a lot, though the user interface was difficult to manage.

Clubhouse is trying to tap in to the same audience that Anchor had, which, ironically, was predominantly people of color.

I joined a few conversations, but I wasn't crazy about the etiquette rules there. While you can join conversations to listen in, it's frowned upon if you offer your two cents unless solicited. As such, I didn't speak in any conversations unless I was asked to join a room.

Clubhouse will be much, much bigger in the future. Is it for me? I'm not sure. I don't have the time to explore a new platform right now, but I'm not ruling it out.

AUTOMATICALLY ADD TO CART
WITH AN AMAZON LINK

An author in a Facebook group shared a tip on how to send readers a link that automatically adds your book to the shopping cart on Amazon. You can do this by creating a special link and appending it with your book's ASIN and a syntax command. I won't share what it is because these things always change, but you can search for how to do it on the Internet.

At the time of this writing, it works quite well and you can add a series to it so that readers can buy an entire series in one link. An excellent marketing tool for your email list!

However, this link doesn't allow for link localization, so you have to build it manually for each Amazon store.

A few volumes ago, I talked about Genius Link, a link localization service that I use and recommend. Genius Link has a feature called Advanced Targeting, where you can route people to different links based on parameters such as their country, device, operating system, and so on. Add to Cart links were a perfect use case for this feature.

I loaded all the country-specific links into Advanced Targeting and created a dynamic link where customers were routed to the proper Amazon store. This way, you only have to give out one link, and you can make it a clean, short link using your domain.

This is a very useful technique to sell more books. You can use such a link on your website, social media, podcast, and email list.

READER SIGNALS

When I wrote my book *Shadow Deal*, I developed a way to test my idea against the market to see how it would perform.

When I looked at comparable books, I noticed that each book gave off certain signals to the reader. When I looked at the most successful books and put all those signals together, I could often get a clear picture of why a book was successful.

I called these signals "reader signals."

Some examples of reader signals include:

- Book title
- Series title
- Number of books in series
- Foreground of the cover, or main character
- Background of the cover
- Font of the book title and author name
- Reputation of the cover designer
- Price (ebook, paperback, audio)
- Formats available
- Headline of the *f*book description
- Body of the book description

- Call to action in the book description
- About the Author section on the product page
- Number of reviews and review average

And so on. Overall, I found around 80 reader signals that I could clearly distinguish, mostly on *the product page alone.*

As an exercise, I looked at my book and defined the reader signals for my new book, *Dead Rat Walking*. How many signals could I match from comparable books?

First, I used the Urban Fantasy Book Database tool that I created that catalogues many different urban fantasy series (over several hundred). Unfortunately, I didn't find any comparable books. Uh-oh, right?

Then I did some Internet searches and also looked for books with a shifter main character similar to mine. I only found one. Another uh-oh. However, I did find books that had minor characters similar to mine. I used some of those as comparables and then broadened my search to find books with similar storylines.

Overall, my search for comparables wasn't a fruitful one. I've been here before, and I know how this movie ends...This series may not do well. But you never know until you publish it.

My early search is a decent indicator that I'm either before my time or I have an idea that is slightly off-market. However, I'm okay with that, and I've adjusted my expectations accordingly.

But I digress. Despite the grim prospects, I was able to still match many of the common reader signals in the urban fantasy genre:

- Title: *Dead Rat Walking* (a play on the shifter trope)
- Series Title: *The Chicago Rat Shifter* (indicates the name of the city in the series, and the type of supernatural character, and the genre)

- Number of books in series: between 3-5 (which is how many urban fantasy readers will want to see before they invest in a series)
- Cover foreground: A human character sitting in a sewer, surrounded by rats (the rats are prominent too)
- Cover background: a graffiti-ridden sewer (Graffiti is a common signal for urban fantasy, especially on famous traditionally-published book covers. A sewer is also very urban.)
- Price: $2.99 for ebook, TBD for paperback, but nothing out of line with what other authors charge

You get the picture. I did this with all 80 signals, tweaking and adjusting wherever the book fell out of line with the market. Note that I did not change the book itself—just the packaging. And despite what I change, the packaging still is an accurate description of what the reader will receive when they read the story.

I'm still early in my experiments with reader signals, but I believe the exercise is helpful if only to get you thinking about how your book aligns with the market.

If you're interested, I did an in-depth analysis in fine-tuning the reader signals for my book *Shadow Deal* as part of my *Writing to Market* course, which you can find at www.author levelup.com/writetomarket

KEYWORD COURSE BY DAVE CHESSON

I learned that Dave Chesson published a course on his Kindlepreneur website on how to select keywords and categories for your books. I was technically still in "Amnesia Mode," so I downloaded the course but didn't get to it before I transitioned away from marketing for a while.

This quarter, I watched the course and took extensive notes. Dave is an SEO master, and learning how he approaches metadata selection is helpful if only to understand how he thinks about it.

While I highly recommend that you take his course (it's only $50 at the time of this writing), here were some of my major takeaways:

- thinking about keywords in groups can be a helpful exercise. When you make a list of possible keywords, group them based on similarity. Then run them through Publisher Rocket to figure out which ones have the best earnings potential. I have always done this the other way around.

- BISAC categories and Amazon categories are not the same. I always knew this, it's more helpful to think about how to map BISAC categories and Amazon categories so that I know where my book will end up. Today, I've just been picking categories and hoping for the best, not really understanding how to change them.
- Amazon SEO is all about continuing to return to basics. It's always changing. The techniques I have been using were out of date.

I won't share any more because I believe you should buy the course. I plan on using the detailed lessons I learned with *Dead Rat Walking* so I can give the book the best possible chance to succeed.

NEGLECTING MARKETING

Last quarter, I was hyper-focused on marketing. I discussed my "Amnesia Mode" project, and how I learned many new marketing tips and strategies. I also discussed how I grew my sales with Amazon Ads. Overall, those efforts were successful.

This quarter, I haven't been marketing at all. At least not for my backlist. I have been more focused on book production, setting my strategy for the coming year, and a new editing data and analytics project that I will discuss later in this book. I've also been focused on my final semester of law school.

I've neglected my marketing. That said, my sales are still doing pretty well, and they are slightly up.

I've learned over the past few years that you don't have to market your work every day, or even every week. Sometimes you can get by with less than that, but you'll only get by. Eventually, the numbers do drop off.

I've been trying to find ways to be more consistent with my writing and marketing. I find that I "seesaw" between them. When I write, I write with all my force. When I market, I market with all my force. I do both in short bursts. So far, it has worked well, but my system is flawed. It breaks down after a few months when I realize how long I have *not* been doing the other thing.

I don't know the answer to the problem, so I'm just articulating it here. Perhaps a step in the right direction is to hire people, but I'm not convinced that a marketing assistant will materially improve your sales. I believe that an ad manager could, but for reasons I'll discuss later in this book, that's not technically possible right now.

This got me thinking about ways to automate and outsource your marketing so that even though you're not doing it every day or every week, it feels like you are.

My mind went first to social media, which is what most people do—hire a social media manager. Frankly, I've never had much of a presence on social media outside of YouTube, and I don't intend to change that.

My mind went second to ad management, and third to...nowhere.

Neglecting your marketing is normal when writing isn't your full-time job. That's where I settled this matter for now.

ILLUSTRATED COVERS: THE PANACEA FOR ALL PROBLEMS?

I discussed the looming cover designer shortage in the World-Class Content Creator section.

Another problem with cover designers is finding the right designer for your needs, especially if your character is a person of color. It's difficult to find models of color on stock photography sites. Sometimes you can find good models, but there aren't enough images of that person to sustain a series. As a result, many cover designers who work exclusively with stock images can't help authors in this situation.

The answer? Get an illustrated cover. It's more expensive, but you won't have to worry about the stock photo issue. You also won't have to worry about character poses or backgrounds.

Illustrated covers are trending in fantasy in particular and have been for the last few years. I decided to give it a shot. I'll share how it works out and if creating one had an impact on my sales.

In the next chapter, I'll share a unique problem with illustrated covers that you'll want to consider if you decide to purchase one.

BOOK COVER ADVENTURES

Sometimes you get that feeling in the bottom of your stomach that you screwed up, like you made a misstep that will cause you trouble in the future.

That was how I felt when I got the cover design back for my newest novel, *Dead Rat Walking*. The designer did a good job illustrating the image—no concerns there. But I couldn't help but feel déjà vu.

Upon seeing the cover, I was taken back to the book cover for my book *Eaten: Season 1*, which was probably the worst cover I've ever designed. I'll share more about that cover later in the book, but the gist of that cover was that I confused the designer and wasn't clear in what I wanted. It was my fault, not his.

This time around, I did *not* confuse the designer. We were both aligned around the concept. I also did not overwhelm her with information—I was thoughtful in how I presented the concept, giving her enough direction while letting her do her thing. She did exactly that.

Yet, I still kept feeling like something was wrong when I saw the final cover for the first time. I couldn't pinpoint it. I spent the better part of the day thinking about it.

For starters, when I put the cover on a Pinterest board next to other top-selling urban fantasy covers, it didn't measure up. The scale of the character was too small, especially at the thumbnail level. He didn't stand out.

The typography didn't work either. It screamed post-apocalyptic, not urban fantasy.

The color scheme was too dark. The cover wasn't bright enough.

All signals were pointing toward trouble, and none of it was the designer's fault. I kept thinking that I should have done a better job thinking of a concept that would sell the cover more, although I spent a fair amount of time doing market research and thinking about the cover and how to make it fit within the market.

So I did what I always do when the cover isn't working: I worked with the designer to fix it. I voiced my concerns and gave her specific bullet point feedback on what I wanted to change, using the market as the North Star.

I juxtaposed the cover on the Pinterest board in several different positions and took screenshots so she could see how it stuck out.

There were only two possibilities:

- We'd make the design work.
- We wouldn't make the design work.

Again, this wasn't on the designer. This was on me. If the second scenario came to pass, I considered an unfavorable but possible option: I could hire a separate person to do the typography once we fixed some of the layout and composition issues on the illustration itself. This would add an extra expense to the project (and the series), and I didn't like that option. But that's always a risk you take with illustrated covers. Sometimes the illustrator nails the image but bombs the typography.

Anyway, we got the cover to a good spot. It's still not 100 percent where I wanted it to be, but it gives off the right signals.

I don't trust my emotions, though, because sometimes the cover is just fine and there are other issues that sink a book.

If I ultimately fail, the lesson I learned the hard way with this project was the importance of character scale. That will be one of the first requirements I discuss with the designer next time. If you screw up the character scale, you screw up the entire cover. Scale is everything on urban fantasy covers. If anything, it should be bigger than normal. You live and you learn.

Additionally, for the next cover, I'm giving the designer an action scene to illustrate. And that scene will be in a bright setting so that the cover stands out. That will make sure I don't end up here again.

Time will tell how well I steered the designer on this project. She was fantastic and I will be working with her again, but I've published too many books to make these kinds of mistakes. I'll do better next time.

WHAT BEING REJECTED FOR A TED TALK TAUGHT ME

In the last volume, I discussed how an opportunity to apply for a TED talk came up suddenly, and how I rushed to apply for it.

I was rejected.

Around the beginning of the year, I received a form rejection. I wasn't selected for the role, or even to be an alternate for the role.

It was a tough blow. I've wanted to give a TED talk since the first time I saw one, and I thought I had put good preparation into the application and my demo video.

But these things happen. I thought about it for a day and permitted myself to be a little down. Then, the next day, I moved on.

Why did they turn me down? I have no idea, but it was probably because my pitch just wasn't the right fit for what they were looking for.

I always have to remind myself about a story that happened to me early in my career.

I once applied for a job that I wanted. I wanted it so bad that I was envisioning myself in the role already because it was such a perfect fit for me. My interview went amazingly well, and I thought for sure I'd get the job.

I didn't.

I was crushed. Devastated.

I found out later that the hiring manager was a narcissistic jerk. The person that got the job instead of me ended up leaving the company in disgrace because the manager was impossible to please.

If I had gotten that job, I would have been miserable and it would have dead-ended my career.

I got another job several months later that wasn't nearly as glamorous but opened the door for me to double my salary in just a few years.

Yeah, fate.

Ever since then, I learned to be grateful for the jobs I got, and especially grateful for the jobs I didn't get.

The same is true with rejection.

Be grateful for the times you are accepted, but be especially grateful when someone turns down an opportunity to work with you. Even though it's painful, it's probably for the best.

Rejection still stings nonetheless, but I always remind myself of that story any time I face a hard rejection.

What did I learn from the TED experience?

1. I can pitch like my life depends on it, and it may even help.
2. I can prepare a pretty good pitch in 24 hours if I need to.
3. Sharing about the application publicly was a little embarrassing since I didn't get the role, but maybe someone learned something.

When one door closes, another one opens. Right around the

time I received the TED rejection, I received an acceptance to write an article for *Writer's Digest* magazine. The magazine's acceptance and the TED rejection were within days of each other. It's funny how that works.

That's why I try not to let rejection bother me too much. It's just a numbers game.

I've accumulated thousands of rejections for opportunities that have come up in my writing career. The TED talk rejection is just another badge of honor on my writer's journey.

BECOME A TECHNOLOGY-DRIVEN WRITER

AI, BLOCKCHAIN, AND VIRTUAL WORLDS

Joanna Penn published a book titled *Artificial Intelligence, Blockchain, and Virtual Worlds: The Impact of Converging Technologies On Authors and the Publishing Industry.* I always buy Joanna's books on launch day, and this one didn't disappoint.

Joanna has been a pioneer in the emerging tech space for authors for years, building her business on the back of emerging technology. Not only was this book different than what she normally writes (in a good way), but it was a masterclass in building thought leadership in a space that she already dominates. I highly recommend that you pick up the book; it is quite short at around 60 pages, but it gives you a lot to think about for the future of your author career.

I've said for a long time that self-published writers will need to adapt to the times. The techniques that made us successful today are not going to be the same techniques that make writers successful in 2030. This is because of emerging technology, the rapidly changing publishing industry, and reader tastes. Joanna keenly understands this and has done great work in shepherding writers into the future. This is one of the reasons I admire her so much.

Here are my takeaways from the book:

- The future is here now. It is not something that is coming. Many of the technologies that Joanna talks about in the book are nascent, but they do already exist.
- The future belongs to writers who understand copyright. There will be amazing opportunities for writers who understand licensing and contracts. For example, licensing your voice into a voice double can be a lucrative endeavor if you understand how to negotiate the terms.
- AI as co-author is an interesting future. Imagine writing a book with the assistance of an AI that knows everything you have ever written, your book sales, what your readers want, and how to write just like you. What kinds of amazing work could you create?
- Blockchain isn't quite there yet, but it has the potential to completely disrupt and disintermediate the ways that authors are paid. Out of all the technologies in the book, this one seems the least far along, but when it reaches a watershed moment, it will be a big deal.

I won't share any more of Joanna's tips because you should read the book.

LESSONS LEARNED AFTER BUYING A STANDING DESK

I finally bought a standing desk. I've been saving up for the last few years. I didn't want to settle for an easy solution—I wanted to buy a real standing desk with all of the benefits.

I bought a desk from Uplift.com, which I highly recommend. It took about two hours to put together by myself, and the instructions were simple to understand. The desk also came with a smattering of accessories that improve its functionality, such as cable management clips, zip ties, a tray for hiding your cables, a magnetic sleeve for routing your cables, and even tabletop grommets with outlets in them.

When I was done setting up, I had the best workstation I've ever had in my entire career.

People have been asking about my setup, so here it is:

- Uplift desk with two grommets: one with two power plugs and another for wire management.
- A 36-inch monitor to use as my main screen, and a laptop stand to prop up my laptop.

- A Mac docking station that has ports for USB, Ethernet, HDMI, and SD cards to save ports on my laptop.
- A surge protector underneath the desk in a wire tray that powers my monitor and desk.
- Lots of clips, zip ties, and hooks that route my cables around the desk and keep everything off the floor.
- A magnetic surge protector that clips to the side of the desk that powers additional items that I may need to unplug from time to time, such as my laptop and lamp.
- Velcro straps with adhesive strips that secure my external hard drives and podcasting audio interface underneath the desk, out of view. I can simply attach and reattach the equipment as needed.
- A wireless charger for my smartphone plugged in under the desk.
- A boom arm for my microphone that swings out of the way when I don't need it.
- A studio light that clams behind my monitor, giving me flattering lighting.
- A headphone hook that clamps to the desk that stores my headphones so I can grab them conveniently when needed and keep them out of the way otherwise.

This is an all-season setup. In seconds, I can raise or lower the desk to a preset height.

If I need to write, I can do so in whatever position I like.

If I need to record a podcast episode, I simply turn on my audio interface, swing the microphone over, open my recording app, and start talking.

If I need to do a podcast or YouTube interview, I swing the

microphone over, turn on my webcam and studio light, and switch on my ethernet connection.

All this, with almost nothing on my desk.

That's why investing in a *real* standing desk was worth it. I couldn't do any of this stuff with my old desk without moving things around and disrupting my office.

Now I don't have to worry about that, and I have a healthier, camera-ready, and more productive writing setup that will be tax-deductible.

DIFFERENT WAYS TO WRITE

A few years ago, I tried Dragon Anywhere for dictation and didn't like it. I felt that the usability and accuracy weren't to my liking compared to the desktop version. I had written it off and didn't think twice about it.

Recently, a reader reached out and asked my thoughts on Dragon Anywhere. Because it had been so long since I used it, I decided to try it again.

I found that the app had improved significantly since the last time I used it. In fact, I liked it so much that I purchased a subscription immediately. Dragon Anywhere has helped me dictate my books while on the go; for example, I am dictating this chapter right now while washing my dishes. Being able to dictate on your phone is practical and a way for many Mac users to access the power of dictation, even though Dragon for Mac has been discontinued.

That got me thinking about all the different ways in which you can write a novel in today's environment.

You can write a novel on your desktop or laptop using a writing app. This is the traditional way of writing.

You can also write by hand. There's nothing wrong with that either.

You can also, as I do, write on your phone using a mobile writing app.

You can dictate your book using software like Dragon, but this does require investment in software and certain hardware.

You can also dictate on the go using Dragon Anywhere.

You can dictate into a digital voice recorder or voice recorder app on your phone and upload the audio to Dragon to be transcribed, or you can hire a transcriptionist to turn your speech into text.

In other words, there is no excuse not to find a way to write and be more productive in today's new world of publishing. The question is how you want to accomplish it.

Instead of saying "I can only write on my computer," think instead: "I will write based on my circumstance at the time." For example, if you are at home on a Saturday night sitting in front of your desk, then writing on your desktop or laptop makes sense.

If you have carpal tunnel or repetitive stress injuries, then it makes a great deal of sense to adopt dictation when you are experiencing pain. If you are at the doctor's office, or in the park, or somewhere where it doesn't make sense to have your computer in front of you, then writing on your phone is a suitable option.

Think about the mode of writing as merely a tool to help you get the writing done.

With the most recent novel that I wrote, I wrote part of it on my phone, part of it on my laptop, part of it while dictating on an exercise bike, and parts of it while standing up and walking around speaking the story.

This is why I believe that this is the greatest time in the history of the world to be a writer. Never before have writers had such unparalleled flexibility in how they choose to tell stories for which readers are willing to pay them.

As I say all the time, your writing app and writing style are the most important early decisions in your career. Your goal should be to find the writing app that fits you like a glove. When you do that, you'll automatically become more productive because you won't waste time arguing with your writing app. Instead, you'll spend your time focused on the nuances of your story.

BACK ON MY DRAGON

Around Christmas, I hurt my back. I was walking my dog and tripped over an uneven part of my driveway. I woke up the next morning looking like the Hunchback of Notre Dame. It didn't help that it was the first week of winter and extremely cold, which is never good for people who have arthritis and back pain.

This happens to me a few times a year. This time was really painful, so much that I had to limit my computer time because it aggravated the pain. Writing on my phone was a godsend that helped me maintain high word counts even in the jaws of pain.

During this period, my wife sustained an eye injury. Thank goodness it was just superficial, but she couldn't use screens for a week. It got me thinking about dictation again and how it's such a valuable skill to have. In fact, I argue that it's one of the most underrated moneymaking skills in today's self-publishing economy.

The average person types around 40 words per minute, but they speak 150 to 160 words per minute. Prose doesn't fly out of their mouth at that rate, but heck, even if you spoke 80 words per minute, that would double your word count.

I wrote about my exercise bike challenge previously in this book, but before that, I remembered my fantasy series *The Last Dragon Lord* fondly. It's my most popular fiction series to date, and it's the first one where I learned Dean Wesley Smith's Writing into the Dark method, and how I learned to write novels in one draft. I also wrote it with Dragon, the famous dictation software.

I remember being so frustrated with Dragon for Mac! It would misunderstand even the most simple words. I had to RELEARN how to speak for it to understand me; ironically, it improved my diction. Dragon also misunderstood proper nouns, which was an exercise in frustration with fantasy. But I worked through that, patiently teaching it how to pronounce almost all the proper nouns in the story.

I hate cleaning up errors unless I have to, so I *forced* myself to use Dragon without ever touching the keyboard. It took several weeks, but I learned how to dictate super smooth and clean prose. It was such a valuable skill that it helped me rack up record word counts.

Unfortunately, a lot has changed since 2016, and I had to revamp my dictation workflow. For starters, Dragon for Mac was discontinued, so I had to buy the Windows version. My investment in running Windows on a virtual machine using Parallels continues to pay off. In just a few minutes, I had Dragon up and running.

And WOW is the Windows version superior in every way. It doesn't suffer from the accuracy issues that the Mac version had. It's also smoother with fewer bugs. I can't tell you how many times I lost chunks of my story in the Mac version because it would quit unexpectedly. That hasn't happened with the Windows version once, and I doubt it will.

So I'm back on my Dragon. It's good to flex my dictation

muscle again. The first day I dictated, I racked up around 1,500 words in about 30 minutes, which is quite slow at 50 words per minute. But I'm rusty and still relearning how to use Dragon. I do not doubt that I can improve my speed to around 80 words per minute once I am more comfortable.

During my exercise bike challenge, my goal was to dictate for at least one hour per day for one month. At 80 words per minute, that's 4,800 words per day *just on the exercise bike.* It doesn't count my time at the keyboard or on my phone, where I consistently write anywhere from 2,000 to 5,000 words per day. I'll let that sink in.

What would happen if you could write between 6,800 and 14,800 words of *clean prose* every single day for the rest of your author career? Good god...That's a novel every week, or at best, every few days. On the low end, that's 2.84 million words every year! That would put you solidly into pulp writer territory, possibly into the top one percent of all writers who have ever lived.

This is how dictation can help you become a technology-driven writer. Dictation serves as a cybernetic of sorts, helping you write faster and become a better version of yourself. And it's powered by artificial intelligence.

Also, remember that other forms of artificial intelligence will disrupt how we write novels. The future belongs to writers who can create amazing stories the fastest, and who have the biggest catalogues. The writers with the most books win. If you have a lot of books *before* the disruption, it'll be easier for you to survive because you'll have access to more opportunities that emerging tech can provide.

What if you could harness the power of dictation and future artificial intelligence to help you write stories even faster? Imagine have a dictation session, going to bed, and letting an AI take over, matching your word count for the day. Then, when you pick up the next morning, the AI reads the story to you, and then you pick up where it left off. Very interesting. We'll see if it's plausible.

THE FUTURE OF WRITING APPS IS ABOUT CONNECTIVITY

I've noticed an increase in emails from developers wanting my advice around creating new writing apps for writers.

I put out a call in 2019 that I'd help any developer who wanted me to review their software and offer feedback. That offer still stands, and in 2020 alone, I spoke to over a dozen developers. Each one surprised me in amazing ways. There are a lot of people working on apps with interesting feature ideas.

One developer asked me what I believed the "pie in the sky" future of writing apps *should* be.

The answer is simple: the future of writing apps should be about connectivity.

Today, you create your book and have to transport it between closed ecosystems. For example, you write your novel in a writing app, send it to Microsoft Word or Google Drive for your editor, reimport it back into your writing app, then export it to software for publication. That's three different ecosystems that aren't connected. And frankly, those ecosystems aren't interested in working together either, which is why they're going to be disrupted and completely irrelevant in the near term.

In Volume 2 of this series, I wrote about the idea of "one command center" that a writer can use to write, edit, and format their novel. The idea was around a single app that is multi-platform and access based so that you invite editors and formatters to work on your book within the app itself. In short, it would function much like the Adobe Creative Cloud does today; you can import and edit Adobe files in different Adobe programs with incredible ease and convenience. For example, I can import a Photoshop file into a Premiere video file and even manipulate the layers of an image while editing a video. That's the type of connectivity and synergy we need in the writing space.

Whoever figures this out is going to disrupt the market. As long as the app continues to evolve, the writing experience is akin to the leaders on the market today and it is available multi-platform with feature parity, writers won't think twice about switching. I even suspect that they'd be willing to pay a subscription.

Imagine an app with the smoothness of Scrivener, the tracked changes ability of Microsoft Word, and the formatting precision of Vellum. All with the ability to invite your freelancers into the book file itself to help you improve it. It's a no-brainer. Hell, freelancers such as editors and formatters might start working exclusively with an app like this.

The good news is that I'm aware of an app that is taking this exact approach and will be launching soon (at the time of this writing). I have no idea if my ideas influenced the developer (probably not), but I'll cover it in a future volume *Indie Author Confidential* when it launches, and if it's as good as I think it will be, I will consider putting my full support behind it. I predict it's going to do very well, and if that happens, the entire writing app market will look entirely different in the next few years.

CATCHING MISSING DETERMINERS

I'll be talking in the next chapter about an editing project I'm working on to help me improve the quality of my manuscript edits.

Part of that project involved reviewing my last five novels and looking for trends in changes that my editor recommended.

One of the trends was missing determiners and prepositions. It's easy to leave "and," "a," "an," "the", "to" and "of" out of sentences. Since determiners are only two characters, they're easy to miss during self-editing, and my editors don't always catch them either. I find that when I'm dictating, I miss determiners at an even higher rate. For some reason, Dragon doesn't pick them up well.

I investigated if there was a way to solve this with a stand-alone application using Natural Language Processing. After speaking to a few data scientists, we determined that it was too expensive and too involved. We also found that Grammarly handles this issue in particular well enough after some testing. ProWritingAid catches them as well—and it catches different ones too.

While I can't say that I agree with everything Grammarly

and ProWritingAid recommend, the fact that they can catch missing determiners is worth using them for that reason alone.

Missing determiners keep me up at night. Despite *me* not being able to see the error, a reader sure can.

If this is a problem you have in your writing, use ProWritingAid (paid) and Grammarly (free). Together, they'll help to minimize the determiner problem.

STITCHING TOGETHER BOOK REPORT AND AMAZON AD REPORTS

If you run Amazon Ads, you need to understand how your ads are performing.

I watch my ads closely, paying attention to the profit and conversion rate to determine if a set of ads is working.

Your profit is determined by the amount of money you make on a book minus the ad spend.

Your conversion rate is determined by the number of clicks your ads receive divided by the net units sold. This gives you a number that is best expressed as a ratio, such as 1:10 or 1:20. The lower the number, the better. My experience has been that anything less than 1:10 is usually profitable.

How do you calculate all of this? Amazon Marketing Services provides one report for your ads, and KDP provides another report for your sales.

I used Book Report instead for my sales. I selected the option to view my sales for the month:

I simply copied the table with my sales and units sold into Microsoft Excel:

Then, I went to the Amazon Ad dashboard, selected portfolio view, and clicked "Export." This works best if you use port-folios and name them based on the book title.

In Excel, I converted the sales data into a table and added a couple of extra columns to the end:

Then, I copied the Amazon Ad data into the spreadsheet just to the right of the table and converted it into a proper Excel table.

Next, I used a VLOOKUP formula to "stitch" the two tables together like so:

And, of course, I did some basic formula work:

When I was done, I had all of my sales and ad data on one table. This took me about five minutes.

In five minutes, I can see how my ads are performing without having to do any data entry. I do this at the end of the month to determine how my ads performed.

AUTOMATING MY BOOKKEEPING

I don't know about you, but I don't exactly enjoy doing my taxes. I also don't enjoy spending several hours each month cataloging all of my receipts for my accountant to review at the end of the year. My time is best spent writing. Yet I do have to run a business. And running a business means keeping good records and staying on top of your paperwork. I find that most of my receipts come to me via email and I find that I do the same things with those emails every month.

So I had an idea: what if I could automate my receipts so that when an email receipt arrives in my inbox, a system could take that receipt, rename it, catalog it, and even fill out a spreadsheet with all the information about the purchase so that I no longer had to do it? (I explored this topic in earlier volumes under the topic of "email parsing.")

It turns out that this is very doable. I purchased a subscription to the service Zapier, which allows you to connect your web services.

I ran a pilot. Since many of the transactions I made are from PayPal, I created a workflow where any PayPal I received that came to my inbox was automatically cataloged and entered into a spreadsheet without me having to lift a finger, based on certain requirements.

Here were the rules and steps:

- If the email was from PayPal,
- mark the email as read,
- move it to my folder titled "Expenses",
- parse the following fields: "date," "amount," and "description", and
- pass the parsed data to a spreadsheet with corresponding columns

The pilot wasn't perfect, but it was a success. All of my December PayPal receipts were entered successfully onto the spreadsheet. I could easily send that spreadsheet to my accountant and he wouldn't bat an eyelash. He wouldn't even know that it was automatically generated. That, my friends, is the definition of efficiency. It will take me a while, but I plan on implementing this with most of my receipts. This will allow me to automate the majority of my bookkeeping, saving me several hours each month, especially at tax time.

LIVESTREAMING WITH OBS

Last year, I started experimenting with live streaming. Every month, I did a "Writing Power Hour" where I invited my community to join me as I dedicated 90 minutes to writing. We wrote together as a community in 20-minute increments, five-minute breaks, and a question-and-answer session at the end for anyone who wanted to ask me writing-related questions.

The power hours were such a success that I will continue doing them for the foreseeable future. However, my streaming setup is quite basic.

Several YouTubers in the writing space are quite savvy at streaming; I spoke to a few of them to ask them questions about their setup and how they stream. All of them pointed me to OBS, which is a free broadcasting software that is easy to use, but difficult to master.

I have the hardware I need; the software is free, but live streaming professionally requires some thought. First, I need an overlay. An overlay is a graphic that has your name, social media icons, a space for your webcam, and a space for any other items you want to share on your screen. In my case, I thought it would be nice to include a timer on the screen for people so that they know where we are in the writing sprint. I also thought it would be nice from time to time to have a space for sharing my screen in case I want to show my audience something.

It sounds like a relatively simple affair, but to do an overlay correctly, you need to have solid branding. Until now, I have not engaged in any branding for "Author Level Up." I have avoided commissioning a logo because I'm not prepared to go down that route yet. I should already have a logo, but it's not needed. If I were to do an overlay correctly, I would have a logo and branding already set. That's why I was a little hesitant to do this. However, I do need to improve my professionalism. I decided to commission an overlay anyway, with the understanding that I am going to have to do this again down the road once I get my branding affairs in order.

Why am I waiting on branding? First, I am in sore need of a new website. I plan on commissioning a logo in getting branding designed when I'm ready to build my new website. That might be at least one or two years from now.

Anyway, I spun my wheels a lot while thinking about improving my live streaming game. Probably too much. But there are always things you have to consider down the road. I should have my overlay situation resolved next quarter, and I look forward to sharing my audience feedback on how my new streaming setup looks.

SMALL JOB PROGRAMMERS

Programming costs are cheaper than you think. You can hire a programmer to solve quick problems for you on a site like Fiverr or Upwork.

Gig sites get a bad reputation, but I've been able to automate many areas of my business and obtain custom solutions to common author problems, all under $100.

I paid an Excel macro VBA programmer to create some difficult macros that I couldn't do myself. It cost me around $280 for a few different jobs. I also paid a developer to write a custom PowerShell script that I also needed for my sales database. That was $85. The result was that I was able to automate my entire sales calculation process, saving me at least four to five hours per month. The $368 I paid is pennies on the dollar compared to the time, money, and energy I got back. Plus, each job only took the programmer a couple of hours, if that.

Another time, I hired a small job programmer was to improve the performance of my website to meet Google standards.

For my editing analytics project that I'll discuss in the next chapter, I hired a programmer to create a custom Microsoft

Word macro that helped me catch repeated words in all of their various tenses because this is a common issue I have when writing.

If you know when to engage them, programmers can help you with a lot of tasks. The key is understanding how the tools on your computer work.

Are you using your computer and your applications' full horsepower? The answer is probably not. But if you can unlock even just a few extra features, it's amazing what you can do.

ZOTERO FOR RESEARCH

My research process is clunky and I need a better tool to improve my productivity.

I realized this when I was researching *Dead Rat Walking*. I was using Evernote, whose Web Clipper is fantastic, but I found that organizing research leaves a lot to be desired.

I did some research and found a free app called Zotero, which is a Windows application that is designed for academics. It allows you to save content from the Internet, organize it, and prepare citations accordingly.

I played around with it and liked it. I'm not sure if it's "the" app for me, though.

It seems asinine to suggest that writers need an app for this. It's just not a priority, and the features of many writing apps such as Scrivener are just fine for most people. But I couldn't help but think there is probably a better way—at least for *me* to internally organize my material so that an app can help me store it.

Another thing about research is that you want to make sure you save your findings forever. You may never need them, but if you write a sequel ten years from now, you'll be glad you did.

I'm not convinced Evernote will be around forever—it seems to be struggling financially these days and its app usability has declined in recent years. So I know that Evernote is not the answer.

I'll keep looking. But Zotero is worth checking out.

CUSTOMIZING MY NEWS FEED
WITH AI

In the Ideas You Can Steal section, I write about an idea for a content curation service for writers using artificial intelligence.

Just for fun, I did some Internet research one evening to see if this type of product existed on the market and whether the technology existed for a layperson to curate content of their choosing.

The answer was not yet, but I did find an interesting way to use artificial intelligence to create a custom blog news feed.

It involved downloading an open-source AI kit, using Pocket (the feed reader service), and a willingness to train the AI by clicking on headlines that you wanted to read. If you did this enough, you would have a custom feed of your favorite blogs, based on articles you clicked on those blogs in the past. It was a crude proof of concept, but a decent one.

I can imagine a future where this type of curation is available for all entertainment mediums, driven entirely by the user. On the Internet, we *already* live in bubbles of our own choosing based on our preferences. It's only going to get worse, but there's a benefit to this too.

With all the noise out there, it can be hard to know what

content to consume. For example, I listen to at least a dozen podcasts. I *want* to listen to every single episode and give it my full attention, but that's simply impossible. I would love a service that DJs the episodes for me, serves me segments it thinks I will like, and then I can choose what I listen to in full, if I listen to anything at all.

I imagine this with books too, beyond what Goodreads offers.

However, the tech has to be easy for the end-user.

As I will discuss later in this book, the company that can solve the discoverability problem will win pretty much everything.

BECOME A DATA-DRIVEN WRITER

MORE EXCEL DATA TRICKS

The more I use Excel, the more I realize it has a marketing problem. It is hands-down the most powerful app ever created. I believe that Excel can help anyone live a better life by helping them make data-driven decisions, but Microsoft bungles this.

Let me give you an example. I've talked at length about how I created a sales database that gives me a nice and clean pivot table I can use to answer any question about my sales.

I track my yearly expenses in a separate spreadsheet (with a pivot table), and I've always thought it would be nice to (easily) track whether a book is profitable or not. In other words, did the book make more than I spent to produce it? This is difficult to do without data entry, and you know how much I hate data entry.

I discovered that Excel has a feature that allows you to tie the data in two or more different pivot tables together so that you can create one master pivot table that contains ALL of the data.

To keep this simple, this means that I can tie the data from both my sales reports and my expense reports into a single pivot table so I can answer the question "how profitable are my books?"

Pretty cool, right? You'd think this would be called "multi-pivot tables" or something easier to understand. Instead, Microsoft calls it a "data model." I can't think of a term that is more frightening to a non-data person like your average writer.

Anyway, I recognize that this chapter may not resonate with you. But know that Excel can do almost anything with data that your heart desires if you know how to speak its language.

AMAZON ALEXA FLASH BRIEFINGS: COLOSSAL FAILURE ON AMAZON'S PART

Amazon Echo devices have become increasingly pervasive in the United States and around the world.

I have several Amazon Alexa devices in my home. A couple of years ago, I thought that they would become all the rage. They have.

I also thought that a new feature that Amazon Alexa devices offered called flash briefings would also become popular. Flash briefings are like micro podcasts that your Amazon Echo device reads to you. My "Writing Tip of the Day" podcast was originally designed for Amazon flash briefings. Only at the last minute that I decide to syndicate the show to traditional podcast channels.

"Writing Tip of the Day" is almost 2 years old at the time of this writing, and it barely gets 100 listens across Amazon Alexa devices per month, despite flash briefings being a major selling point for Amazon Alexa app developers. By contrast, "Writing Tip of the Day" receives anywhere between 3,000 to 5,000 listens per month on traditional podcast channels. It's not even a contest.

Amazon doesn't promote its flash briefings. They don't give

you any tools to advertise them. They aren't discoverable on the Amazon website unless you specifically search the flash briefing store. And most importantly, they don't give flash breathing listeners a good way to rate, review, or share shows that they like. In my opinion, this is a colossal failure on Amazon's part.

Will I stop doing flash briefings? No, because it doesn't take any extra effort. It's just an additional checkbox I select when I upload my audio, so it's not a big deal.

My "Writing Tip of the Day" podcast is the most rated and highly rated podcast on the Amazon flash briefing store in the United States with a whopping six reviews at the time of this writing. Globally, I probably have around 10 reviews. Every other show in my niche has less than that.

I hope that Amazon does something to revise its flash briefing format because it is an untapped opportunity.

URBAN FANTASY MEGA SURVEY

My friend and fellow urban fantasy author John P. Logsdon facilitated a mega urban fantasy reader survey where he and a team of urban fantasy authors asked many questions about reading habits.

(John, Ben Zackheim, and I created the Urban Fantasy and Paranormal Romance Book Database, which is also the best-kept secret in the urban fantasy genre. Just sayin'.)

The amount of data was staggering. Over 800 avid urban fantasy readers responded to the survey.

While I can't share the raw results publicly, I can share some of my key takeaways as it relates to a new urban fantasy series I'm writing.

Eight-hundred readers is still a small sample size in my opinion, and because these readers are primarily followers of self-published authors, there's a strong support of self-publishing that I don't believe would play out the same way if you had a full swath of the general urban fantasy readership. So while there are biases in the data, it's still helpful.

- Seventy-five percent of readers said that the gender of the main character did not impact their reading decision. That seems to suggest, despite female characters being most prominent in urban fantasy, that readers *will* read male-driven novels, and there's a market opportunity that hasn't borne itself out yet. (My new series follows a male hero.)
- Fifty percent preferred the first-person point of view, 34 percent preferred third-person, and 41 percent didn't care. (My series is written in the third-person, which puts it in the minority.)
- Ninety percent of applicants preferred stories with snarky humor. (My story is about a hero and his sister who have a snarky relationship.)
- Seventy percent of readers preferred romantic tension. (My Book 1 doesn't have a romance, but the main character has just endured a bad breakup and is dwelling on it.)
- Seventy-five percent said that they're always willing to try new authors. (My pen name is a new pen name.)
- Eighty-eight percent didn't care if a book was self-published. Two percent only preferred traditionally-published authors. Again, this data is highly biased in my opinion.
- The top three areas where readers find new authors were recommendations from another author, Freebooksy/Bargain Books, and Amazon Ads.
- Fifty-eight percent use Kindle Unlimited.
- Sixty-seven percent said that they'd only start a series if there are five or more books available in it.
- The majority of respondents indicated that the book description was the most important marketing

material they reviewed first to evaluate a book, followed by the type of supernatural character, then the cover, then the book sample.

- Sixty-one percent do NOT listen to audiobooks.

While I admit to cherry-picking the data to use in this article, there wasn't anything in the survey results that put my current series off-market. In fact, my series should fit right in with reader expectations.

The data tells me that Kindle Unlimited is the right choice and that $2.99 is the right price point. It also tells me that audio isn't necessary until or unless the book starts selling well. Then audio is a smart move as more readers get used to the medium in the coming years.

The data also tells me to spend at least 80 percent of my packaging decisions on my book description, followed by the book cover. The book description is *that* important. That's also helpful data for Amazon Ads, because if an ad campaign isn't working, it will probably be because my book description isn't strong enough.

It's not always easy to glean data from readers, but I'll take all the data I can get.

BALANCING WORDS AND NUMBERS

I was in a meeting at work with an individual who bombed me with slide after slide full of numbers that had no context. I had to keep asking, "What does this mean?"

I was in another meeting shortly after that where another individual was presenting a business case for a project. I had to ask "What data do you have to support this case?" because the presentation was based on feelings and emotions, not actual market data.

Most writers are word people. The very thought of working with numbers freaks them out. I know this because I use to be one of those people.

Some writers are numbers people. They can look at numbers all day. When it comes to logical arguments and craft, they're more comfortable retreating to their land of numbers.

The proper place to be is in the middle. Word-focused writers shouldn't be scared of data, but they shouldn't feel the need to be data experts either. Numbers-focused writers shouldn't be scared of the "wordy" parts of writing, but they shouldn't be compelled to be craft wizards.

Just rely on your strengths and seek a little bit of the ground that you're not familiar with.

SMARTPHONE APP DATA: AN UNTAPPED GOLD MINE?

I had a chat with a developer who was talking to me about his process for creating smartphone applications for iOS and Android. He is a developer by trade and has developed some successful apps, one that has over one million downloads.

He showed me what he was working on, which was a great app that helped writers in the writing process.

We started talking about the possibility of creating an app for my community, though nothing serious. Personally, it's not on my to-do list any time soon, but the developer was telling me how the data and analytics of apps are an untapped gold mine.

Essentially, he told me that I could monitor people's habits while using the app. For example, if I embedded my YouTube videos on the app, I could monitor how long they watched my videos, their demographics, and other quirky habits. That's potentially valuable information, though not for me right now.

That got me thinking about the merits of a smartphone app in general. Is it really to create value for your audience, or is it really for the data?

One of my objections against creating a smartphone app is that it's inconvenient. If I wanted to create an app that collected all of my podcasts, YouTube videos, and blogs, it's a lot to ask someone to download that app and use that exclusively. More than likely, they're going to want to listen to me on a podcast app where they do all of their other consumption. Same with YouTube. I worry about that with app development, especially when it comes to selling books directly.

So while that option is not for me right now, it's undeniable that there's a treasure trove of data there if I ever wanted to pursue it.

API ADVENTURES

I believe that application programming interfaces (APIs) are the future. I've discussed APIs in prior volumes of this series, but I'll give another refresher.

In my quest to understand APIs, I took a course on API basics. The instructor gave one of the best examples I've heard to explain an API in simple terms.

You're hungry. You have two options. You can make a delicious meal from scratch or you can go to a restaurant.

If you go to a restaurant, you simply order off the menu, and in a few minutes, a server brings your food.

APIs are like going to a restaurant. Like a restaurant, data that you obtain from an API is easier to obtain, made-to-order, and more convenient than if you created the data yourself.

The second analogy I've heard is that an API is like a plug and socket. The application is the plug, and the data is the socket. When they connect, you get electricity. I like the restaurant analogy better.

An API is how a developer plugs in to existing data.

For example, if you've ever used a social media app and found yourself wanting to use a GIF, you can click a button and access the entire library of a site like Giphy. You can even search for just the right GIF to use without leaving the social media site! That's an API at work. The social media site calls the GIF website, and you can navigate the GIFs (data) accordingly.

To give another example, I use a WordPress plugin that connects to the YouTube API and lets me display all of my YouTube videos on my site. This updates automatically. Users can watch my videos without leaving my website, and I still get credit for it on YouTube. This is a nice convenience perk to make it easy for viewers of my website to engage with my content for the first time. That's another typical use of an API.

APIs allow for increased interactivity and functionality among applications.

They hold so much promise in many areas of the writing life. The biggest areas I have my eyes on in the publishing space are as follows.

Sales data. It doesn't make sense that authors have to download their sales data from a dashboard every month. Most authors are not Excel-savvy anyway and struggle to analyze their sales data in a meaningful way. If retailers offered APIs, a developer could create an app that pulled the authors' sales data into the application, manipulates and analyzes it, and prepares nice charts so that it lifts the burden from the author.

Publishing and publishing updates. Why upload a book to a dashboard when you can just use an API? I foresee the writing apps of the future connecting directly with retailers so that you can write, collaborate with an editor, format, and publish, and maintain your books from the same interface. This will become increasingly more important the more "prolific" authors rise to prominence—authors with dozens if not hundreds of books. They won't have the time or the patience to manage books on a dashboard. They'll want to manage their intellectual property from one place.

Book monitoring. In addition to publishing and updating your books, an API relationship can also help you spot when something is wrong. Maybe you just finished a promotion and forgot to raise your price. Or maybe the HTML in your book description is broken. Or maybe you've published the wrong book! With retailer API access that monitors your metadata on an hourly or daily basis, a developer could create a solution that warns you anytime something is wrong. It could even warn you when your book is selling more than you expected!

App connectivity. APIs can also connect apps so that they can run synchronously. Imagine Vellum interfacing with Scrivener, for example. Or, if you wanted to integrate a special Internet dictionary with your writing app, the writing app could connect with the dictionary. Writing apps don't offer this kind of interfacing currently, but I believe they will.

Author-created APIs. Imagine that George R.R. Martin woke up one day and decided that he wanted to let people write fan fiction in the *Game of Thrones* universe. It's difficult to remember all the characters, history, spellings, and events that happened in the series, so he could create an API that interfaces with your writing app to give you editing assistance *in the moment* while you're writing instead of having to look it up in a wiki. Click an icon of the *Game of Thrones* logo on your writing app menu, search what you're looking for in a pop-up window, obtain the information you need, and keep writing. The interface could even offer spell-checking and basic fact-checking, scanning your manuscript for any misspellings or possible incorrect references to the *Game of Thrones* canon.

There are more creative uses too.

MORE LOVE FOR MICROSOFT WORD MACROS

In the last volume, I discussed a unique way to use Microsoft Word macros for my editing rules engine project. I described Microsoft Word macros as a sleepy, boring topic. More accurately, I said: "No one (except me) wakes up in the morning and says, 'I bet Microsoft Word macros can help me solve problems!' Nope. The very idea of Microsoft Word macros puts most writers to sleep. It's boring, too technical, and they can't see the benefit."

But I found another excellent way to use Microsoft Word macros to improve the accuracy of my dictation.

A major problem with Dragon is that it misunderstands proper nouns. You can teach it some words, but it still struggles if you don't say the word the same way every time.

Another issue with Dragon is that to get the best accuracy, you have to use it with Windows Notepad, which eliminates the ability to do any formatting.

Macros can help.

Every time I wrote during my initial warm-up sessions, I paid close attention to how Dragon printed the word. If the misprint was consistent, I added the word or phrase to a list. I then put that list into a find and replace macro in Microsoft Word. Once I was done dictating, I copied the text into Microsoft Word, where I would run the macro to fix any of the prior issues. Then I copied it into Scrivener, knowing that the text was as clean as I could make it.

I also used the macro to change the formatting of the text to play nicely upon pasting it into Scrivener.

Combine this macro with a rules engine and a good copyeditor and proofreader, and you have a recipe for insane daily word counts and a higher quality story with fewer errors.

IN PRAISE OF PAUL BEVERLEY

I wanted to use this chapter to make more people aware of Paul Beverley, who is, in my opinion, the pre-eminent world expert in Microsoft Word macros.

Paul is an editor in the United Kingdom who has created over 800 macros to assist editors in editing their clients' work.

I don't know any editors who use Word macros because, frankly, it's an acquired taste. However, Paul published a free book and dozens of videos on his website to help people understand why they are important. He also does training sessions. His macros are free.

While Paul's target audience is editors, there's no reason *writers* can't use his macros.

When I first discovered Paul's work a few years ago, I will admit that I couldn't "see" how macros could help me. I didn't even know what a macro was at the time.

It took a few years for things to "click," and now that they have, I believe that Paul is an underrated gift to the writing community.

Here are a few of his macros:

1. ProperNounAlyse produces a list of all the proper nouns in your story so you can tell if anything is accidentally misspelled.
2. HyphenAlyse scans your story for any words that should be hyphenated.
3. Duplicate Words highlights every instance of a duplicated word, such as "said said" or "she she."
4. Comments Exporter exports all of your editor's comments to a table so you can review them all together.

And more.

But perhaps the most powerful tool Paul created is a macro called FREdit.

FREdit is a scripted find and replace. Let's illustrate its usefulness with a common problem that Scrivener users have.

For some reason, Scrivener doesn't handle curly quotes consistently. Sometimes it puts the quotes facing the wrong way —especially if you use them after an em dash. It's maddening.

If you wanted to eliminate this problem manually, you could search for an em dash followed by an open quote, replace all with an em dash followed by a close quote.

Or you could load these characters into FREdit and it will catch them every time, along with any other error you want to catch.

Maybe your next book won't have the weird em dash issue. Then FREdit will simply skip it as if it didn't exist, and move on to the next issue.

So FREdit basically acts as a storage engine for your errors and flags them any time they show up in your writing.

I hope you can see now why this is so powerful, and why it is now an indispensable part of my workflow moving forward.

We have Paul Beverley to thank for his macro brilliance. Check out his website at http://www.archivepub.co.uk/book.html.

THE RISE OF EDITING ANALYTICS

Sometimes I venture down rabbit holes that seem odd. If you made it this far reading this series, then you probably know what I am talking about.

The topic I'm going to explain next may seem like one of those rabbit holes, as the next several chapters explore different aspects of it. However, I want to reiterate my mission as a writer: to entertain my readers in the niches I write in, and to remain nimble in an ever-changing industry.

Everything I do daily is about adding value for my readers and removing roadblocks. The most obvious example of that is writing books and marketing, but that's not the only example. Improving your productivity means more books for your readers to enjoy. Managing your business expenses and streamlining them means more money in your pocket at the end of the year that you can reinvest back into your business, which helps readers. Unlocking data and analytics in your writing business means you can find ways to deliver better value to your readers and delight them more. Adopting emerging technology means that you can be there when readers' habits and preferences change, which they almost certainly will.

So everything I do as a writer, marketer, and business person, is about adding value for my readers.

I can think of no better way to add value for your readers than to learn how to tell better and cleaner stories. Readers love a book with minimal typos, but they also love a book that doesn't have plot holes or obvious craft errors. These are invisible expectations that they don't explicitly ask for, but if you don't deliver, they'll let you know all about it. Therefore, every writer has a vested interest in learning how to produce cleaner manuscripts consistently.

In the writing community, we're addicted to writing productivity. Everyone wants to know how to write faster. At the time of this writing, "word sprints" are popular— where people try to write as many words in a single session as possible while worrying about editing later. National Novel Writing Month (NaNoWriMo) is a challenge where writers all over the globe try to write a 50,000-word novel in November. Writers are adopting dictation at a rapid rate to speak their stories at higher word counts. The common advice is to release a new book every few months so readers don't forget about you. In short, everyone wants to know how to write like a machine and reap the benefits.

This isn't new. In the good old days, pulp writers made a living writing fast. There were pulp writers who wrote more in one month than some writers wrote in their lifetime. So the inner desire to write fast isn't a new phenomenon.

But what about writing fast *and* cleanly? In other words, just because you write 5,000 words per day, how clean is your manuscript when you send it to your editor?

In my opinion, editing quality is the other side of the equation. As a practical tip, I'm not a fan of writing fast and sloppy. I believe it's better to do it right the first time.

When you send your book to your editor, that's the ultimate test. It tests both your writing and self-editing skills.

If you write 5,000 words every day, that's great, but how many errors is your editor finding? If it's a lot, you might want to do something about that because it's probably costing you.

I'm not telling people to slow down. In fact, I think you should write as fast as your brain and fingers allow. Rather, I'm suggesting that it's worth it to take some time to think about how you can improve your self-editing so that you can send squeaky clean manuscripts to your editor.

The writers who write fast *and* ship clean manuscripts win. It's the pinnacle of efficiency. How good are you at both sides of the equation?

This has been on my mind a lot lately. I write quickly but find that my editor often corrects the same type of mistakes in my manuscripts. I do my best to avoid repeats, but I can't remember every single edit she recommends.

I want to avoid making repeat mistakes, as that would save my editor time, reduce my editing costs over time, and result in a better product for my readers.

In previous volumes in this series, I wrote about the concept of an "editing rules engine" and natural language processing artificial intelligence for writers, and how I believe these are viable solutions to easing the burden of self-editing while still producing a cleaner manuscript.

I believe that writers can use the power of data and analytics to help them write better stories. Your story is nothing more than a series of data points, and so are the edits your editor recommends. I believe that this data tells a story (but not of the fiction variety), and I believe there is a logical way to analyze it to gain insights into how you can become a better writer. I also believe you can approach this problem with technology and automation so that you don't have to do it manually (which would be too time-consuming).

I call this concept "editing analytics"—using data and analytics during the editorial process to help you improve your story.

Most people think of editing analytics in terms of statistics: your story has X adverbs, is X words long, and so on. I've never found that helpful because statistics don't help you tell better stories. Just because you have 100 adverbs in your manuscript doesn't mean readers will care. They probably won't. Same with your sentence length, or silly things like ending a sentence with a preposition. Fixing your book based on these types of "analytics" will hurt your story, not improve it.

Artificial intelligence programs such as Grammarly compare your work against the writing of millions of other users and make recommendations based on edits of other users' work. This is also not helpful. (Grammarly is a helpful service, but it can only help you find last-minute typos, not help you become a better storyteller.)

Editing analytics is about using analytics from YOUR work (and YOUR work only) to gain insights into how to become a better writer. It's about discovering errors that you shouldn't be making so you can prevent them in the future. It means looking back on the editing data of a few of your novels so that you can be more proactive.

(Developmental editing is out of scope here. We're talking strictly about copyediting and proofreading.)

As I said before, your book is full of data points that are untapped and underrated. To develop an editing analytics mindset, you need to think about your story as a series of data points, not a story. This seems counterintuitive, but it's similar to thinking about your book as a product. When you transition your thinking, you'll see opportunities where others see chunks of written words.

This quarter, I finally made significant progress toward creating a prototype for my editing rules engine. My 30th novel seemed like a good place to start; it's the first book in a brand new series and it's the first novel I wrote with mixed writing methods. I wrote it on my laptop, Scrivener iOS on my phone, via dictation while sitting down, standing up, on an exercise bike, and while doing chores. I also wrote the book quickly—in about 21 days. I amassed 61,000 words from a diverse array of methods, and I wanted to know how clean the manuscript was for my editor.

For example, dictation tends to be a sloppier writing method because programs like Dragon frequently misunderstand you. Might it be true that dictated sections in my novel trigger more edits from my editor? Would those edits be spelling and grammar-related, or story-related? Maybe it's true that dictation leads to more continuity-type errors. I don't know, but I can find out using editing analytics. It could also be true that dictating a chapter has no impact on the number of edits I receive.

Let's not forget that our books go through self-editing, and that muddies the data somewhat, but the question stands: how good is your writing and your self-editing, and can you improve them?

The key is to focus on *what* triggers edits. Maybe there's something you're doing unconsciously that your editor has to keep correcting. Maybe there are trends you can find in your manuscript by looking at your edits differently. You won't know until you dig deeper.

That's why I believe that editing analytics is an incredible opportunity because it can help you be a better version of yourself.

MORE PROGRESS TOWARD MY
EDITING RULES ENGINE

I built a prototype of an editing engine to help me deliver cleaner manuscripts to my editor.

Here was my process before the pilot:

1. Write the book
2. Send the book to the editor
3. Receive edits back
4. Learn a few "takeaways"
5. Write the next book and hope that I didn't make the same errors

The result was I continued to make repeat mistakes, and I missed many of the lessons my editor caught in earlier books.

With the editing engine pilot, I added additional steps to the process:

1. Write the book
2. Send the book to the editor
3. Receive edits back

4. "Score" the manuscript to see how many edits I received and how many edits could have been prevented
5. Teach selected edits to the editing engine so that it can recognize them
6. Write the next book
7. Run the manuscript through the editing engine so it can identify similar mistakes that would have been "repeat" mistakes
8. Send a cleaner manuscript to my editor

The result is fewer repeat mistakes. It also saves my editor time and allows them to focus on other more important issues in the manuscript—issues that only an editor can find.

The first step in building the engine was to create a chapter-scoring engine.

When I look at an editor's edits, I want to know a few things:

- How many edits did they recommend (as tracked changes)?
- How many comments did the editor make on the manuscript?
- What is the breakdown of those edits (spelling and grammar versus continuity and story)?
- How many edits did I receive per chapter?

That's a basic picture that you can glean from your edited manuscript with the right tools. You can accomplish this in seconds with automation in Microsoft Word.

The real insights are at the chapter level.

I created a tool that I called a "chapter-scoring model." It sounds fancy, but it's simple: it looks at several data elements present in each chapter and then gives each chapter a score based on how well it underwent my editor's scrutiny.

The model is based on both objective and subjective factors. The data elements for the chapter scoring are:

The total number of spelling and grammar errors. These usually take the form of tracked changes on a Word document. These are the most important edits in the editing engine because you can teach the editing engine to spot them using code.

The total number of continuity and story-related edits. These usually take the form of comments in your Word document. Editors are usually hesitant to change a story issue, but they will point it out. Some comments, however, are spelling and grammar-related, so I filter out comments that don't meet these criteria. Also, I can't teach continuity edits to the editing engine. These are uniquely in the editor's territory.

The total number of spelling and grammar-related edits and continuity and story edits. This is perhaps the most telling number. A chapter with a higher number of total edits means it required more of the editor's attention, which is a bad sign. It's not all bad, though—you get good data and can learn a great deal!

The number of writing sessions per chapter. A chapter with a higher number of writing sessions may indicate more errors, especially if those sessions are spread out over several days. On the other hand, a chapter written in one session may not necessarily be better either.

Duration of chapter creation. If you start writing a chapter in January, suffer writer's block, and don't resume writing until March, that may indicate that more errors are present, especially of the continuity type, since it may take some time to remember the story.

Writing method. Some forms of writing are cleaner than others. Trust me, I would know. I find that text written by hand on my computer tends to be the cleanest, followed by text dictated while seated at my desk, followed by words written on my phone, and so on. Words I dictate using Dragon Anywhere always require the most corrections in self-editing.

Mood while writing the chapter. I believe mood is underrated. My theory is that if you feel good when you're writing, you'll produce fewer errors, but it could also be true in certain instances that being in a state of "flow" produces more errors because you're not thinking about spelling and grammar when you're getting the words down.

These components work together within the model. For the prototype, I gave them all equal weights.

The next step was to determine a baseline. Sure, I want to track the number of total edits, but what is "normal" for me?

Fortunately, I save all of my edited manuscripts and leave the edits untouched so I can refer to them later. I've done this with all 50+ books I've written because I knew they would come in handy one day.

Using a Microsoft Word add-in, I took my last five novels and counted the number of total edits and edits per chapter. This took about five minutes. My results were surprisingly consistent from book to book, even with different editors: between 275 and 400 total edits, with about 7 to 11 edits per chapter on average. I have no idea how that stacks up against other writers, but I can at least tell you that readers rarely complain about errors in my books.

Using my averages for each objective category, I used that to create a scoring system based on a five-point scale with the average in the middle.

For example, my average number of edits per chapter is nine. If I receive less than nine edits per chapter, that component scores more favorably. If I receive more, it scores worse. I performed a similar exercise with the other components so that every component has a score associated with it.

Then I simply created a spreadsheet to capture the data for each chapter with the scoring working behind the scenes.

The lower the score, the better. With a simple sort, I filtered the chapter scores to see how they ranked. I started with the chapters with the worst scores to see what the drivers were.

With one test chapter, I noticed that the number of edits was well over the average. In examining the chapter, I found that it was a fast-paced chapter. The editor made a lot of comments around continuity and paragraphing. I had a healthy amount of grammar errors too. While this is only one chapter, it could be an indicator that other fast-paced scenes may score similarly. If that's true, then I can start looking to the future by spending more time on these chapters when I self-edit my next novel to see if I can bring that number down. I might also want to bring this to my editor's attention. Therefore, the existence of a fast-paced scene becomes an indicator that I can also track at the chapter level. Not only do I have backward-looking data that tells me they're a problem, but I also have forward-looking insights that I can use to reduce my errors.

I also discovered that one particular error was showing up again and again in my chapters—repeated words within a small radius. For example, I used the word scream four times on one page, which was painfully obvious to my editor. I'll discuss how I tackled this problem in the next chapter.

But the scoring engine showed me a tremendous amount of insights, even with a limited demo that didn't utilize the entire engine. When it's time to send my 30th novel to my editor, I predict that it will teach me a lot. It will also test some assumptions I have, such as:

- Sections written while in a good mood generate fewer errors in editing.
- Writing on my phone doesn't produce any more noticeable errors in editing than writing on my laptop.
- There is a relationship between the number of spelling and grammar edits and the number of continuity edits in a chapter (I just don't know what they are).

Once I receive the manuscript back from my editor, I will score it using the methods I just described. Then I will review the spelling and grammar errors in each chapter to determine which ones could have been prevented if I could have taught them to the editing engine.

For example, I can solve the repeated word problem. That accounted for 12 errors in the first five chapters *alone*. That's an entire chapter's worth of edits! Imagine what your editor would say if they reviewed an entire chapter and found no errors...

Another example of an error that the engine can catch is a misused word. One time, I used the word "cadence" incorrectly when I should have used "interval" instead. I can teach the engine to search future manuscripts for every instance of "cadence," and if I use the word, generate a comment with a warning to check the usage of the word. The comment can even include the sentence I got wrong in a prior novel, just to show me how I screwed up in the past. Microsoft Word's Editor, Grammarly, or ProWritingAid can't catch these types of errors. I can do this with a Word macro (Word macros aren't so sleepy after all!) that can be written in just a few minutes. The macro code is identical for virtually any word I use incorrectly. I can also do this with hyphenated words, or words that should be hyphenated, and if the edit is black-and-white, I can have Word just find and replace the offending item. Any changes will show up as a tracked change!

Another common example that I mess up frequently is numbers. Any number under ten should be spelled, and any number over ten should be expressed as a numeral. Also, my editor recommends spelling out percent instead of using a symbol. I can program the macro to catch these types of errors.

These errors seem obvious, but you'd be surprised how easy it is to miss them. Programming them ensures that you will always catch them and that they never are a problem for you ever again. The more edits you teach the engine, the more comprehensive it gets.

Once I teach the editing engine a slew of edits from the editor's recommendations, I can count those edits, subtract them from the overall scoring, and then see how the chapters score. I can then express the difference as a percentage, and say with confidence that, for example, "If I had run the manuscript through my editing engine knowing what I know now, it would have resulted in a manuscript that had 16 percent fewer errors." That's powerful.

Then, with your next book, you can run the manuscript through a slightly modified version of the scoring engine, and, using indicators (like fast pacing) you can potentially *predict* which chapters will pose the most problems for your editor. If you wanted, you could flag those chapters for your editor as a heads-up.

In a sense, the scoring engine can become a predictive model, especially if you pair it with natural language processing. Using something like this with artificial intelligence would be like pouring gasoline on your analytics. My prototype only utilizes Word macros, but there's an entirely different universe of edits that would open up if I integrated this with natural language processing, namely the ability to catch more sophisticated errors that a macro can't catch, such as dropped articles, which are the bugbear of authors and editors everywhere.

There's so much to explore here.

In an earlier volume of this series, I wrote about a fictional app called Shapeshifter that will be the writing app of the future. Providing editing analytics in addition to writing analytics is one way that such an app can help writers become a better version of themselves.

ELIMINATING REPETITIVE WORDS
FROM MY FICTION

My editor has to constantly correct a particularly pesky problem in my manuscripts: I repeat words too much within a short radius. For example, I used the word scream four times on one page and didn't realize it. My editor found other similar instances throughout the novel. Thank goodness she caught that!

That got me thinking about how I can prevent this problem in the future. For starters, no writing app or advanced spell-checking app I know of can catch this problem. Yet it feels like something that can be addressed programmatically. Your writing app can search for a word...why not create some additional logic around it?

I reviewed every instance in the manuscript where my editor pointed out repeating words, and I noticed that the repeated words always happened within a 100-word radius, usually between 5 and 25 words. The most extreme case was 81 words.

My gut told me that I was onto something, so I posted a job and had around a dozen or so developers look at a sample of my work, examining the problem.

Turns out that Microsoft Word macros can help me (again!)

I spoke with a developer who said that he could write a macro that would take the following steps:

- Analyze all words within a 100-word radius.
- Highlight every instance of any repeat words within the radius.
- Proceed to the next 100 words, and repeat.

The macro would sweep through the entire manuscript. The developer also promised to build me a filtering tool where I could add words I wanted to exclude, such as common words like prepositions, pronouns, dialogue tags, proper nouns, and so on. The only thing he couldn't help me with was perfect tenses of words, like break/broken. It would have been too difficult for him to program every word. I considered that to be a fair compromise.

A week later, the developer sent me a Microsoft Word user form macro that worked quite well.

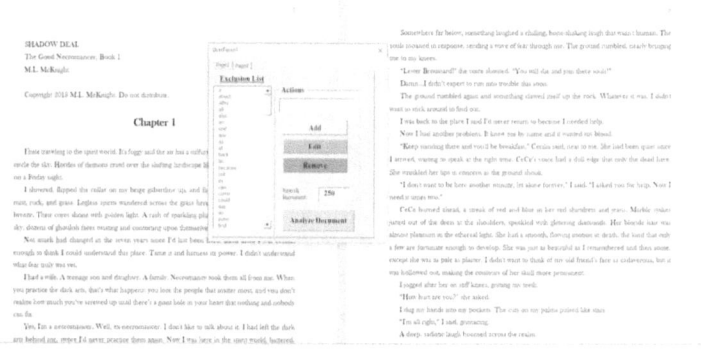

The developer created a Word userform that allows me to add words to an exclusion list that I DON'T want to check for, as well as change the increment of the repeats. It also has a separate tab where it will show me a list of all the repeated words so I can easily determine if I need to add new words to the exclusion list.

When I run the macro, it highlights every instance of repeated words, using colors to help me identify frequency.

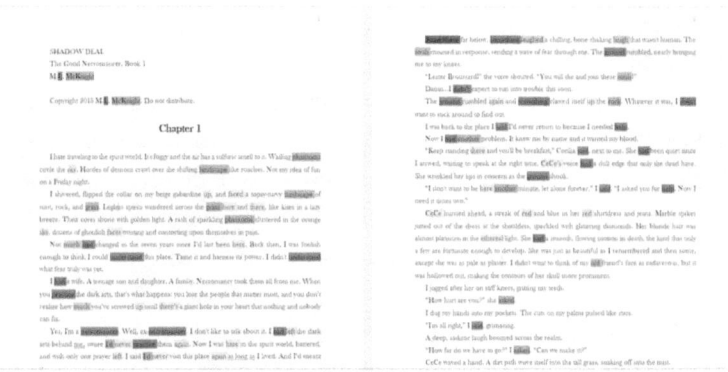

I can look at a page and tell instantly by color where the repeats are. I'll admit that it took some getting used to, but I adjusted to it quickly.

In reviewing Dead Rat Walking, I found at least 100 instances of often-repeated words that needed to be fixed. Leaving them would have presented poorly. I'll let that number sink in...

For example, I used the word "water" seven times on one page. Not only would ebook and print readers have noticed, but it also would have sounded terrible in the audiobook edition! I found a way to cut my usage of "water" down to around three times.

I also discovered words that I repeat regularly. So many of my repeats were "face", "ground", "up", "down", "dark", and so on. I would say that around 80% of the issues I caught involved the same words. That's insightful because I can now create a separate macro that looks for overused words and highlights them separately so I can view them in isolation. That would allow me to add them to the exclusion list on the repeated word macro so I can focus on the uncommon repeats. Over time, I'll keep refining this so that it becomes stronger.

It took me around six hours to sweep my manuscript for repeated word issues, and I caught a lot of them. But I probably missed some, and that's okay.

It's also worth noting that sometimes repeating a word makes sense and it's the only option. I didn't replace every single repeat—that would have been silly. I merely looked for ways to say the same thing a little differently so that it wouldn't trigger the reader to say "he just repeated that word five times in a sentence." The edits were minor, and even subliminal at best.

Anyway, this was a huge success, and one of the more effective parts of my new editing workflow.

APPLYING EDITING ANALYTICS TO MY NOVEL

Since I've spent a lot of time in this volume covering the editing analytics project, I figured it would be a good idea to share some early results.

I'd like to share the results from all the chapters above.

TRACKING MY EDITS

I keep all of my editing documents, so I reviewed my last five novels and categorized the edits. I used macros to count how many edits I received, which gave me:

- The average number of total edits (spelling+story). My average is 290 edits per novel.
- The approximate number of total edits per chapter. My average is 8.5 edits per chapter (based on 50K).
- This is approximately one edit per 177 words for an average of novels that are 50,000 words. Ideally, you want this number to be as high as possible.

And yes, I'm sharing these numbers out of transparency. No idea how I stack up to other writers, but you can certainly compare your numbers to mine.

Anyway, these numbers became my baseline.

Then I went through each novel, looking for anything I could teach to my macro set. This took me about two hours, and I found approximately 150 items that I could train the engine to catch reliably.

I ran the manuscript for *Dead Rat Walking* through the workflow to test everything.

THE NUMBERS

In two minutes...

The workflow caught 178 errors.

I accepted 166 of those errors. Sometimes the engine isn't always right. Still, 166/178 is a 93 percent success rate.

(The errors that I accepted were all, without exception, items that my editor would have corrected. This isn't theory. It's practical.)

Since Word counts double when counting many tracked changes (due to insertions and deletions), I divided this number by half to get the closest approximate number of "actual" edits, which was 83.

The engine also caught seven additional duplicate words that did not show up as tracked changes.

The engine also caught seven errors that Word likely would have captured if I had spell-checked the document prior. I did not, mainly because I was curious how much Word's spell-checker would contribute to the errors caught.

I also caught two errors by eye as I was glancing through the manuscript.

That brings the total number of errors to 99.

99 errors / 38 chapters = approximately 2.36 errors per chapter

Word caught 7 out of 99 errors, which is seven percent of the overall total. So if you ever wanted to quantify how much Word contributes to a book's manuscript quality, that's how you do it. A seven-percent error capture makes Word spell-checker essential in my opinion.

PRETEND WITH ME FOR A MOMENT

If my editor usually catches an average of 290 total edits per novel, and I captured 99 of those edits before I sent my novel to her, that means the engine (probably) reduced my total edits by 34 percent.

If my editor usually catches an average of 8.5 edits per chapter, and the engine catches an average of 2.36 (spelling and grammar) edits per chapter, I reduced the number of edits per chapter by 25 percent.

The reduction numbers get even better when you consider that the numbers I tracked include both spelling and story errors. If you look at just the spelling/grammar edits by themselves (which I didn't do due to time), it's an even more drastic reduction.

Also, the repeated word part of the workflow isn't turned on yet, so that will account for more errors caught next time.

And Grammarly and ProWritingAid both would each catch somewhere between 6-12 errors if I had used them. So I could have been looking at 120-130 actual errors caught, and that's on the conservative side.

The more errors I take off my editor's plate, the more she can focus on other things that may be hiding in plain sight. In other words, the more errors I find ahead of time, the more errors she can find after the fact because they'll "stick out" more.

As you can see, this starts adding up in a very big way. All with free tools, just a little bit of programming costs (my choice), and an understanding how to use the full horsepower of the technology that's already on your computer.

BECOME THE WRITER OF
THE FUTURE

PICK TWO SKILLS TO MASTER

My first real job was as a proposal development specialist at a web development company. This was in 2007 when businesses finally realized that they needed websites. I'd accompany the CEO to meetings with local businesses, listen to small business owners describe their business needs, and then I'd prepare a proposal that included a timeline and a price.

As we prepared for a meeting one day, the CEO said something once that was groundbreaking to me at the time: "The client can choose between speed, quality, and price, but they can only pick two."

Of course, this is a mantra in business, but I had never heard it before.

Speed.

Quality.

Price.

Clients could buy a cheap website that we developed quickly, but the quality would be lacking.

Or they could buy a high-quality website that we'd develop quickly, but it would cost them.

What does this have to do with writing? Nothing at all. But it has everything to do with being a writer.

In the first *Kingdom Hearts* video game, the main character, Sora, has to pick two skills that he will master in battle throughout the game. He has three choices: strength, magic, and defense.

He can master strength and magic, but he'll have bad defense, leaving him open to higher damage from enemies.

He can master magic and defense, but his strength will be lacking.

Or he can master strength and defense, but he'll never be good at magic.

This is a similar metaphor to the speed, price, and quality choice. I believe it applies to being a writer.

Writing.

Marketing.

Business.

Pick two. Or rather—figure out which two you're inherently good at.

Whichever two you pick, you'll always trail behind with the one you don't choose.

For me, I'm a decent writer and I understand business. But marketing has always been my Achilles' heel.

Some writers are great at marketing and business, but their writing needs help. Others are great at writing and marketing, but they have no business skills and do things like sign terrible contracts or burn through their money.

It's up to you to figure out what your top two skills are. You may never master the third, but you can improve your proficiency in it over time.

FACING SELF-DOUBT: THE ONLY BATTLE THAT MATTERS

I receive emails from writers weekly who battle with self-doubt.

They are afraid of starting their books, or they can't seem to finish.

Many of them are quite successful people. Executives, entrepreneurs, or people who have a lot of experience in an industry.

Yet when it comes to writing a novel, they freeze up.

In their personal or professional lives, they would have no problem conquering an issue. They wouldn't hesitate to make a decision. If something needs to be done, they do it.

But in the world of a writer...

It's a big problem. I've dealt with self-doubt too. The only way I escaped it for good was having a near-death experience (which I don't recommend).

The answer to the problem is so simple yet so hard for most people: keep going. Self-doubt tries to fool you into thinking that you can't finish your book, or that you're a terrible writer. The thing about self-doubt is that while its *words* are sharp, it can't take any *action* against you. Its power comes from its words, but when you decide that its words have no power over you, it can do nothing. Then it gets *really* scared and says even more horrible things to you. It'll dig deep into your childhood and fling insults at your like you've never heard before. That's because it's scared. When you turn it into a cornered animal, it will lash out.

And then, in that moment, when you stand firm in your decision that its words have no power over you, you win. Self-doubt will evolve to challenge you again, but the matter of you becoming a writer is settled. If you can get that far, things become easier. Not "easy street" by any means, but easier.

If you want to become the writer of the future, you have to become a writer. Winning the war against self-doubt is what separates long-time professionals from amateurs.

WHY CHASING NOTORIETY LEADS
TO DESTRUCTION

I read a depressing article on Slate about women and the notability problem on Wikipedia. I didn't know that a supermajority of articles on Wikipedia is about men. The Wikipedia community has strict guidelines on who receives coverage on the website, requiring sources that imply "notability," like newspaper articles, magazine articles, and prestigious awards. Because women don't get their fair share of coverage and recognition in these places, they don't receive nearly as many articles on Wikipedia, even though they are just as deserving if not more than many of their male counterparts.

What was particularly depressing about this article is that Wikipedia doesn't seem interested in making any changes to their guidelines. How many times a week does the average person use Wikipedia and not even know about the website's blatant bias against women? People of color? Other minorities?

This got me thinking about how authors chase notoriety and how it's a futile effort.

So many authors want prestigious awards, coverage on television, newspaper mentions, and other traditional media outlet spotlights. They believe that this coverage is critical, and it becomes a barometer for how successful they are.

Who doesn't dream of having their own Wikipedia page? There used to be a seedy group of individuals on a social media group who conspired to get each other Wikipedia coverage. Sometimes it worked, and sometimes it backfired. But getting a Wikipedia page was so important to these people that they were willing to bend ethical rules to get it. I always thought it was pointless.

Self-published writers are the opposite of "notable" in the mainstream sense of the word. Traditional publishers scoff at our existence. The newspapers that do cover us generally aren't friendly. Don't even think about television or cable news coverage. The authors who infiltrate these media outlets are usually disappointed. Yet despite this, legions of authors still think that traditional media is required to legitimize their careers.

If you can't get a Wikipedia page, how the heck are you going to get coverage in traditional media?

This is why I say that chasing notoriety (or, rather, notability) is a fool's errand. Be careful what you wish for because you just might get it.

The article reinforced one of my core beliefs, which is to focus on myself and what I can accomplish. If that happens to attract traditional media, so be it. But you can live a great life and have a wonderful writing career without ever being featured in a newspaper. And you can sell a lot of books without some big-name critic gushing about your book.

AMAZON AND RETAILERS ARE NOT EVOLVING

Self-published authors are becoming more sophisticated every day. Many have transitioned into publishers and packagers of content, publishing the works of other authors. Other authors have become so successful that they are running full-time businesses with employees.

Amazon and other retailers are still treating authors like they did in 2010, with the assumption that an individual account is sufficient for most authors' needs.

I've struggled to understand why retailers don't allow authors to delegate access to their dashboards. Retailers should allow only authors to access their account and financial information, but designate access to other individuals who can assist them in managing their books, with the ability to review and approve actions and even revoke access immediately if needed.

Long-term, I'd like the ability for an assistant to review my books to make sure nothing is amiss, and I'd even like to grant them access to sales data *without* granting them access to my bank data, for example.

For an author who runs a full-time business where an assistant helps them with day-to-day operations, this would be a godsend. It would also be a godsend for a place like Amazon Ads, where an author could grant access to a marketer who can manage ad campaigns. Yet none of this is possible today, and it doesn't seem to be on the horizon any time soon.

If more than one person signs in to an author's account, it will flag security algorithms, so even if you can manage it, it's a dangerous proposition that can get your account canceled.

As we move into a future where authors are becoming more sophisticated and successful, I'd like to see retailers evolve too. I would be fine with paying for these features if that's what it took.

THE POWER OF PICKING THE RIGHT PEOPLE

So much in life boils down to picking the right people.

In the writing life, this means hiring the right editor and cover designer. "Right" is subjective, but for me, the right person does what they say they are going to do when they say they are going to do it, gives you a quality product that indicates they treated your work with care, and they offer a drama-free experience. I have zero patience for drama.

For my latest novel, I hired fact-checkers to assist me in validating the research for my book. I needed to fill six positions and posted them on Upwork. Within hours, I had dozens of proposals, far more people than I could hire!

As a former hiring manager at work who was responsible for hiring and firing people, with a pretty good track record of hiring good talent, I am methodical and ruthless in my hiring process. I weed out candidates quickly.

I had three jobs:

- two fact-checkers to review the Chicago scenes in my story

- two fact-checkers to review the rodent biology in the story (the novel features rats prominently)
- two female readers to read chapters with the hero's sister to verify how well the female readers will respond to her

Here are my criteria for any job:

1. Does the person have the skills to do the job?
2. Does the person have the will to do the job? In other words, what signals show me that they want it?
3. Are there any red flags?

For the Chicago fact-checkers, I had two requirements:

- The person needs to either live in Chicago or have lived there for a long time, preferably with knowledge of the Logan Square neighborhood.
- They had to describe their Chicago background.

Without exception, almost all of the applicants were Chicagoans or people who lived there for at least five years or more.

As I reviewed their proposals about their qualifications and why they wanted the job, I paid careful attention to:

- Red flags in their responses. I looked for anything that seemed odd. With a platform like Upwork, sometimes people will say anything to get a job. Sometimes they even post stock language to every proposal. Those people always receive hard no's from me. Once you weed those people out, you usually have a lot of good people left.

- Their enthusiasm. A lot of freelancers found the job intriguing and unusual compared to their usual gigs. One freelancer even offered to visit locations in-person and take photos and videos of the areas so that I could make the writing even more realistic. I like to reward genuine enthusiasm.
- Their track records on the platform. Anyone with a history of bad performance received additional scrutiny. Is the bad performance something they did or did they catch a bad break with a crazy client? There are lots of crazy clients out there—I know that first-hand, so I have some sympathy. First-time freelancers were acceptable.

Ultimately, I selected a Chicago native who lived on the south side his entire life and a northwest-sider who lived in Logan Square for a long time. Both met the deadline, offered detailed feedback, and gave me exactly what I needed. No hassles and no drama.

My rodent biology job was tougher. I needed someone who had a biology degree or who had extensive experience working with rats.

I received proposals from people on the platform who were qualified—a fair number of doctors and seasoned biologists. One candidate worked in pest control. However, the struggle was finding someone who I thought could convey biological details to me in a format I could understand, and who would give me information that I could use in the story. There was also a language barrier with some candidates. I only hired one person who met my criteria, and he was one of the more unusual candidates who, on paper, didn't meet my criteria. He didn't have a biology degree; however, he went to school for biology and worked with rats for a long time but decided he wanted to do something different with his career. He did editing on the side. He ended up being the perfect candidate because he gave me scientific details but in a format I could use.

I found the other fact checker elsewhere. I prefer not to settle when hiring people. Settling always leads to trouble.

The female beta readers also went smoothly. I was looking for:

- a female who had a younger brother
- who could give me feedback on whether the female character in my story was believable or not.

I ultimately selected two candidates who told me stories about their relationship with their brother that were most like the relationship in my novel. One delivered me good, detailed feedback. The other ghosted me after I hired her, so that was a pain. I hired my third choice, who delivered good feedback in a couple of days.

Sometimes you hire bad fits. Sometimes you should have seen the red flags earlier; other times, there's no way you could have known the person would be a bad fit. That's what happens when you engage with so many random people. Sometimes you pick 'em wrong. That's just how it goes.

But when you pick the right people for projects, it makes the projects go smoother. You also do a service to your readers because you make their experience more enjoyable, especially in the case of editing.

LESSONS LEARNED AFTER 50 BOOKS

I recently celebrated publishing my 50th book and 30th novel. That got me thinking about lessons I've learned since I wrote my first book back in 2013.

I thought it would be fun to share 50 lessons, one learned from each of my first 50 books.

Lesson #1: *How to Be Bad/Magic Souls*. Success didn't come as early as I thought it would. It still hasn't come. I thought I was going to be a bestseller by the end of my first year. Thank God I didn't because I would have made egghead mistakes.

Lesson #2: *Reconciled People*. Some books just can't be improved upon. This short story collection is routinely at the bottom of my book sales each year. I've revived sales somewhat with Amazon Ads, but the book is what it is, and for what it is—a literary short story collection—it's a good testament to my storytelling skill at the time I wrote it. Sometimes books are your own personal monuments.

Lesson #3: *Theo and the Festival of Shadows*. This novel taught me how to be more strategic with my spending. After hearing a podcast interview with a successful self-published author, I thought it would be a good idea to purchase several hundred dollars' worth of book promotion ads to improve my book sales. Never mind the fact that the book was selling maybe one copy per week. I lost all of that money. I sold around 85 copies of the book at 99 cents, resulting in a whopping $29.75. I only received a small number of reviews from the campaign too. It was one of my biggest early failures, and hard to justify losing that kind of money with a baby on the way.

Lesson #4: *Callback from the Muse/Muse Poems*. My first poetry collection. These poems are my earliest published writing, written between 2009 and 2010; I wrote this collection for my senior project to complete my English degree. I received an A on the project and graduated with honors. That said, self-publishing a poetry collection was unusual in 2014 and ahead of its time. However, publishing this collection was a lesson in repurposing content. Since I had already written the poems, it cost me nothing to compile them because they were already edited. I bought a premade cover for $40, and it was an easy way to add another title to my name. Even to this day, I'm always thinking about how I can repackage content to add value to my readers.

Lesson #5: *Eaten: Season 1/Food City*. This is probably the novel that defined my early career. It was about a group of terrorist vegetables attempting to take down an empire of processed foods. That sentence alone turns heads and raises eyebrows, but the book cover was godawful. I don't blame the designer; it was entirely my fault because I confused him. I didn't understand what genre the book was in, and I didn't understand what made a good book cover. I micromanaged the design too. The result was a confusing mess that became a black eye on my author brand for a long time. The unfortunate part is that the story itself was well-received. But the idea was so unusual that readers didn't take a chance on it. This book taught me what it feels like when you utterly and completely fail at your marketing.

Lesson #6: *The Indie Author State of the Union* (2014 *edition*). This was my first nonfiction book and a spiritual precursor to the *Indie Author Confidential* series. Every week, I saved the top news articles from the self-publishing community, summarized them, and offered my opinions on them. I compiled those opinions in this book. It was my way of learning about the industry because it forced me to pay attention to publishing industry news. The book sold almost no copies, but it helped me learn rapidly.

Lesson #7: *Eaten: Season 2/Salad Days*. Because of the cover conundrum with Book 1, I tried to salvage the situation by designing my own cover. Ironically, my poorly designed cover was light-years better than the professional one I paid for, but the series still sold no copies. The book taught me that I have no business designing my own covers, but that one day I might have to.

Lesson #8: *Nutrizeen*. This was a novella in the *Eaten/Moderation Online* universe, told from the perspective of one of the main characters, a milkshake scientist named Geoffrey Foster who is the architect of the processed foods' empire and cruelty toward vegetables. He has an awakening and flees with his children to become a good guy and start a new life. The story is told as an autobiography. While I enjoyed writing it, *Nutrizeen* helped me uncover all sorts of world-building problems with *Eaten/Moderation Online* that I had to go back and fix. I unpublished the book because it raised more questions than it answered. This is only one of two books I've ever unpublished. I swore that I would never make such egregious world-building mistakes again, a lesson I carried into my next series, *The Last Dragon Lord*.

Lesson #9: *Indie Poet Rock Star*. This was my first "thought leadership" book. After self-publishing my own poetry collection, I wondered why more poets didn't do the same. I looked across the industry and predicted that within five to seven years, they would. I wrote a manifesto on why poets should consider self-publishing, how to do it, and how to build websites and market their work. Seven years later, many of the predictions I made in *Indie Poet Rock Star* came true. Self-published poetry is mainstream now, with traditional publishers trying to imitate the self-published look. *Indie Poet Rock Star* also landed me on the radar of Orna Ross, founder of The Alliance of Independent Authors (ALLi), which was an important connection for me.

Lesson #10: *Android Paradox (Android X, Book 1)*. This was my first taste of success. I managed to tell a fun, fast-paced science fiction story about an android and his human engineer. *Android Paradox* sold a decent amount of copies in the first year, and the audiobook version was also well-received—my first fiction audiobook. The book taught me the value of tapping in to your readers to figure out what they want.

Lesson #11: *Android Deception (Android X, Book 2)*. This was the first sequel I ever wrote, and my first taste of what writing a series felt like.

Lesson #12: *Android Winter (Android X, Book 3)*. This was the first Book 3 I ever wrote, and the conclusion to my first series. Much like *Android Deception*, I learned how to write a series with this book.

Lesson #13: *Indie Poet Formatting*. This book is a companion to *Indie Poet Rock Star*, and it teaches poets how to format poetry collections for ebook and print using Scrivener. To write this book, I had to become a book-formatting expert. I credit this book with teaching me many advanced formatting lessons that I would carry with me throughout my career.

Lesson #14: *Interactive Fiction*. This book teaches writers how to write interactive novels in my unique style. I wrote it primarily to catalog my thoughts and preserve my process. I also credit this with being the only book to date that lost me a writer friend. A fellow writer took something I said in the book personally, even though I wasn't writing about them. I learned that the words I write have power—and sometimes your words can alienate people, even though that's not your intention.

Lesson #15: *The Indie Author State of the Union* (2015 edition). The second book in the series. It taught me how to prepare for releasing a book at the same time every year. I launched both books in this series in December.

Lesson #16: *Old Dark* (*The Last Dragon Lord, Book 1*). *Old Dark* was a unique idea—the story of a bloodthirsty dragon lord who survives an assassination attempt and wakes up 1,000 years later in a future ruled by his enemies. It was also the first book that I learned to write without an outline, using Dean Wesley Smith's writing into the dark method. It was also the first novel I wrote almost exclusively using dictation and writing on my phone. I relearned how to write while writing this novel, and it paid off in a big way. It taught me that no matter *how* you write a story, readers will buy it if it's engaging. Once I wrote "The End" on this novel, I was never the same—my writer's brain was completely broken and I was hooked on dictation and writing on my phone. *Old Dark* was also the first novel where I hired a cover designer to create unified branding for all my novels moving forward, which was a big step in the right direction for my author brand.

Lesson #17: *Old Evil* (*The Last Dragon Lord, Book 2*). After I wrote this novel, I broke the news to my editor at the time that I used dictation and writing on my phone. She didn't believe me at first because the story was just as clean as what I usually sent her when I typed by hand. That taught me that it doesn't matter how you get the words down—if you self-edit and hire the right editors, readers won't know the difference.

Lesson #18: *Old Wicked* (*The Last Dragon Lord, Book* 3). Finishing this series validated that I learned my lesson from *Nutrizeen* by creating a successful fantasy world that felt real. I used many techniques from *Nutrizeen* in the entire Last Dragon Lord series, culminating in *Old Wicked*.

Lesson #19: *Death Marked* (*Modern Necromancy, Book* 1). This was the first book in a series I co-wrote with my friend Justin Sloan. Just co-writing a novel in and of itself successfully is an important lesson in coordination, communication, copyright, and contracts.

Lesson #20: *Death Bound* (*Modern Necromancy, Book* 2). The first time I wrote a love interest in a story, including a kiss. Actually, Justin wrote most of it—but I learned a crash course in writing a little romance!

Lesson #21: *Death Crowned* (*Modern Necromancy, Book* 3). The lesson we learned in this book was that if your cover designer uses stock photography, to make sure that they have enough images of the model to sustain your series. My designer gave us a great cover for Book 1 and 2, but when we got to Book 3, she had to use a different model for the hero. It's very noticeable. That experience taught me to be more involved when the designer is scouting models ahead of time.

Lesson #22: *Android Poems*. My second poetry collection. I submitted all the poems to literary magazines, and one of them was published, netting me a modest payment. That process taught me how to submit my work to literary magazines like a pro.

Lesson #23: *Honor's Reserve* (*Galaxy Mavericks, Book* 1). Oh boy, where do start? The *Galaxy Mavericks* series is a multicultural space opera, with the first seven books following a new main character. This book was the first book in the series, about a member of a force called The Galactic Guard. The hero rescues people who are stranded in space. I had never written space opera before. While I had a basic understanding of astrophysics, I had a lot to learn. I did extensive research in this book: astrophysics in particular. I also researched the United States Coast Guard because they inspired the armed forces in the book. I hired a fact-checker who was a career Coast Guard member, and the Coast Guard-inspired sections passed muster. However, my astrophysics did not. Readers ripped the book apart for this reason. While *Honor's Reserve* was as good a story as I had written up until that point, the science was so bad that readers put it down. I was always a little embarrassed by the book until I finally worked up the courage to hire an astrophysicist, who read the book and validated my worst fears. It wasn't all bad, though: I realized that if I had hired him (as a fact-checker) before I published the book, *Honor's Reserve* probably would have done pretty well. It's something I plan to do for the entire *Galaxy Mavericks* series. I always felt like I never gave it a fair shot. *Honor's Reserve* taught me the importance of fact-checkers, a lesson that I was finally able to master with *Dead Rat Walking*, which I have discussed extensively in this book.

Lesson #24: *Phantom Planet* (*Galaxy Mavericks, Book 2*). This is the second book in the series, but I wrote it first. *Galaxy Mavericks* is the first series that I wrote out of order. Out of nine books, this is the order I wrote it: 2,1,4,3,5,6,7,8,9.

Lesson #25: *Zero Magnitude* (*Galaxy Mavericks, Book 3*). Once in a dozen novels or so, you stumble across a book that flows off your fingers so well, it seems like it came from heaven. In a surprising bout of inspiration, I wrote *Zero Magnitude* in seven days. It holds the record for the fastest novel I've ever written.

Lesson #26: *Garbage Star* (*Galaxy Mavericks, Book 4*). Another book with an interesting concept, but bad science. It's unfortunate because this novel explores new territory that I hadn't written to date—the dynamics of a multi-generational family.

Lesson #27: *Solar Storm* (*Galaxy Mavericks, Book 5*). I wrote this book backward just to see if I could do it. The book begins in the present, but each chapter steps back in time so you see the making of and unraveling of the hero, who is a cyborg antihero. The reader experiences the story backward, even though they are reading the book forward, if that makes sense. I wrote this book front to back too, so I had no idea what would happen as I went back in time. An all-around fun novel that ends in a way I didn't expect. It taught me the importance of having fun with your writing. *Solar Storm* was also my 20th novel.

Lesson #28: *Rogue Colony* (*Galaxy Mavericks, Book 6*). A novel with a sympathetic heroine who could have benefited from having her book be earlier in the series. That's one of the downsides to writing into the dark with a series this big that follows multiple characters. I have since learned how to manage this better.

Lesson #29: *Orbital Decay* (*Galaxy Mavericks, Book 7*). A main storyline told through the perspective of the series villain. The novel taught me a lot about writing villains.

Lesson #30: *Planet Eaters* (*Galaxy Mavericks, Book 8*). This is the book where the six heroes finally band together to fight the series villain. The book was a masterclass in joining seven storylines together without continuity issues. I aimed high with *Planet Eaters*, and whether I succeeded or not, I learned how to deal with little issues that make a big difference in the story, such as switching point of views, when to use certain point of views, and how to keep all the main characters top-of-mind. The book was a juggling act, and in some respects, one of the most difficult novels I've written.

Lesson #31: *Horizon Down* (*Galaxy Mavericks, Book 9*). The final book in the *Galaxy Mavericks* series, and the final nail in the coffin of a series that was doomed from the start. I wrote nine books in the series, only to ever sell a few dozen of the first three books. I believed in the series idea, and I don't regret writing it, but I made so many tactical errors. It taught me that I had so much more to learn and experience as a self-published writer. I frequently call *Galaxy Mavericks* the nadir of my fiction career. Nothing I ever wrote has been worse in execution. However, the lessons I learned from this series are a multitude that is hard to articulate. I wrote this series in nine months, which took the better part of a year, but by most accounts, that's incredibly fast. I also managed to secure cover designs for all the books in that period, which was also a major feat given how long it takes to get on a designer's calendar. The entire series was a masterclass in learning how to be efficient as an author. This was also the first series I formatted in Vellum, making my paperbacks more professional. After experiencing so much success with *The Last Dragon Lord*, this series taught me how nothing is guaranteed, and that every novel you write is a clean slate, for better or worse. Also, this series bumped me into the 30+ book club. The covers benefited from the unified branding that I established with *The Last Dragon Lord* series, and for the first time, my books finally had cohesion and my portfolio started to look good visually. The designer who did the covers for this series redesigned many of my earlier covers as well. Overall, the several thousand dollars' worth of "tuition" I paid to publish this series helped me mature as a self-published writer.

Lesson #32: *Be a Writing Machine*. The book that changed my career in so many ways, which was such a stark contrast after *Galaxy Mavericks*. This book is my process of writing fast and being efficient as an author. I learned that people love hearing about writers' processes and their personal experience. I never thought in a million years that people would buy the book, but it became a sleeper hit.

Lesson #33: *Dream Born* (*The Dream Mage, Book 1*). My first foray into urban fantasy, and a more down-to-earth, traditional series that followed one point of view. This series made a big statement by putting a black woman on the cover—something I had not seen on fantasy book covers until then. Now it's a lot more common. Story-wise, *Dream Born* is what you'd expect from an urban fantasy, and it taught me a lot about the urban fantasy genre, which I came to like a lot, so much that I decided to keep writing in it moving forward. However, there was a lot about the genre that I missed—if I had set the novel in a real city, it might have done better. Instead, the city was loosely inspired by Chicago. I learned that urban fantasy readers prefer real cities.

Lesson #33: *Nightmare Stalkers* (*The Dream Mage, Book 2*). Another "once in a dozen" novel. I wrote this book in eight days, and it was the most fun I've ever had writing a novel.

Lesson #34: *Evil Waking* (*The Dream Mage, Book 3*). This is the only book I've written that addresses racism. I don't think I did it justice, but it was the first time I wrestled with it directly on the page. I learned that it's not easy.

Lesson #35: *How to Write Your First Novel*. I did extensive market research for this book to figure out how to position it. I read a lot of comparable books and dissected what I thought made them successful, and what they might have been able to do better. This reverse-engineering process worked quite well, and it served as the basis for how I decide to write my writing self-help books.

Lesson #36: *Shadow Deal* (*The Good Necromancer, Book 1*). My attempt at "writing to market" but in my own way. I wrote this book in public, sharing my progress every day in a free course. I also shared my process of research, writing, self-editing, hiring alpha readers, editors, cover designers, and even marketing. This is also the only book where I completely wrote "what I knew." It takes place in my hometown of St. Louis, Missouri, in a neighborhood I spent a lot of time in, and with characters inspired by family members and friends. *Shadow Deal* is a different kind of story in that regard, but I built on several lessons I learned while writing the *Magic Trackers* series, namely how to give my hero a distinct voice and how to portray black characters on the page.

Lesson #37: *Mental Models for Writers.* Another flex in thought leadership. I used the market research techniques I used with *How to Write Your First Novel,* adapting the "mental model" theme for writers. This book landed me on "The Creative Penn" podcast with Joanna Penn a second time. I explore *a lot* of ideas in this book.

Lesson #38: *The Indie Writer's Encyclopedia.* I learned that you can write an encyclopedia/dictionary hybrid and it will sell. I'm still shocked when someone buys a copy. It aims to teach writers all the terms they need to know to be a successful writer. This book is uniquely suited to my personality, which is why it worked. It taught me the value of doubling down on your personality.

Lesson #39: *The Writing Craft Playbook, Volume 1.* Another thought-leadership book, and my first successful lead magnet for my writing books, after many attempts. This book taught me how to write a good lead magnet and dramatically increased my email list.

Lesson #40: *150 Self-Publishing Questions Answered.* I wrote this book with The Alliance of Independent Authors (ALLi), using the immense amount of data they have about self-publishing. I've talked about this book in prior volumes of this series, but it was a masterclass in using data and analytics to drive your content. All the chapters were pulled directly from the most common questions on the ALLi blog and podcast. I also narrated the audiobook for 150 *Self-Publishing Questions Answered,* which taught me how to produce clean, ACX-approved audio.

Lesson #41: *Indie Author Confidential, Vol. 1.* The inaugural book in this series taught me the value of documenting your experience. The topics are items that I discuss on my "Writer's Journey" podcast every week. I believe that if I become a successful writer, the value of this series will increase tenfold, especially the more books I publish in it. I also wrote this book during the beginning of the pandemic, and I'll always be grateful to it for giving me something productive to focus my anxiety on during those difficult first months in 2020.

Lesson #42: *Indie Author Confidential, Vol. 2.* This book focused a lot on my sales database adventures, which taught me how to distill a difficult concept and make it relatable. It was very hard to discuss my sales database project with people without their eyes glazing over. This book helped me collect and organize my thoughts.

Lesson #43: *The Reader's Bill of Rights.* This book helped me reconnect with my readers, and why I'm a writer in the first place, which is important to remember the longer your career becomes.

Lesson #44: *The Author Income Problem.* I outlined my manifesto around a sales database in this book. In many ways, this is an indirect descendant of *Indie Poet Formatting* and *Interactive Fiction.* It takes a difficult concept and tries to walk authors through how to solve it.

Lesson #45: *250+ Writing Tips, Volume 1.* I turned an entire year's worth of my podcast, "Writing Tip of the Day" into a book to make it more useful to my audience. Another lesson in repackaging content.

Lesson #46: *The Indie Author Bestiary.* My first attempt at blending fiction and nonfiction. The book takes the biggest struggles of the writing life and transforms them into mythical creatures, which is an unusual concept. The story is told in the second person present tense, which is surprisingly difficult to do when writing a self-help book when you're telling a narrative. I aimed big with this book and I felt like it did what I needed it to do.

Lesson #47: *The Indie Author Atlas.* I hired an illustrator to create maps for my book. This is the first time I worked with an illustrator.

Lesson #48: *Beach Poems.* This is a poetry collection I wrote in 2016 but haven't published yet, mostly due to forgetting about it. This book is a constant reminder to not sit on your work!

Lesson #49: *Reaper's Way (The Good Necromancer, Book 1.5).* The first novella I ever published. That is a unique honor in and of itself.

Lesson #50: *Dead Rat Walking (The Chicago Rat Shifter, Book 1).* This book is a testament that every book you publish teaches you something. While I don't know how *Dead Rat Walking* will perform, if it does well, it will be a validation that you CAN be successful if you keep learning and evolving. If it doesn't do well, I'll learn more lessons from it just the same.

There you go. Those are 50 lessons I learned after 50 books. I look forward to the next 50!

WE LEARNED RESILIENCE

I was talking to my sister and we were discussing virtual learning and how difficult it has been for our kids to learn during the pandemic. She made a good point: sure, they didn't learn as much math and science as the state wanted them to, but they learned how to deal with all the craziness of 2020. They learned resilience. That's underrated. Meanwhile, a lot of adults lost their minds.

We all learned something in 2020. Even writers.

If you are still writing after all the insanity that has transpired, congratulations—that's a badge of honor. If you didn't write during this pandemic, but you believe in your writing dreams so much that you're reading this book, you get the same badge of honor—it's no less remarkable a feat that you're still here.

Anyway, we all need reminders sometimes of how difficult a time like this is. The whole world is in a pressure cooker.

Ways to stay productive and focused during this time:

- Acknowledge that it's okay not to be okay right now. Then take care of your mental health.

- Keep writing, if you can. Even if you can't afford to publish right now, the act of writing will keep you grounded. The act of writing itself costs nothing, and if you're in hard times due to all the stuff going on right now, you can always publish later. Or publish and get it edited later.
- Find ways to channel your emotions into productive habits. This is why I am doing crazy challenges throughout the pandemic (beast mode, amnesia mode, exercise bike challenge, etc.). It keeps me focused on the writing and off the news.
- Keep finding ways to be grateful and have fun with your writing. You'll do better in all areas of your life if you can find a way to stay centered emotionally, though we will all struggle from time to time.

If anyone needs the kick in the pants to start writing again, maybe this will be it for you. Scary to think about all the writers out there who will never pick up the pen again because of this pandemic. Not just because of loss of inspiration, but also because of health and death.

The rest of us will still be here, still writing and going after our dreams long after this is over, and it will be because we all learned something during this difficult time—how to keep going even in the face of impossible odds.

Keep writing and, as Dean Wesley Smith would say, keep having fun.

THOUGHT LEADERSHIP IS LIKE
SENDING A MESSAGE IN A BOTTLE

I've learned over the years to publish my thoughts publicly. Sometimes you never know what will happen.

Let me give you two examples.

First, in 2014, I published a video called "Drift." It was about how I use writer's block as a way to become a better writer. The video maybe got a few hundred views at most. Fast forward to 2021, and the Editor-in-Chief at *Writer's Digest* watched it and it prompted her to reach out to discuss a collaboration. Out of the 300 videos I've published, one of my worst-performing videos led to an opportunity. Wow.

Second, in 2015, I published a book called *Indie Poet Rock Star*, which was a book that taught poets how to take advantage of the self-publishing boom, something that was barely on poets' radar at the time. That book caught the attention of Orna Ross, who is the founder of The Alliance of Independent Authors, and an avid poet herself. That led to a mutually beneficial professional relationship, and helped me meet movers and shakers in the industry. All because I wrote a book that people would have advised me *not* to write at the time because there wasn't a market for it.

That got me thinking about what type of opportunities await for content that I'm creating today.

Writing is like sending a message in a bottle. Some bottles take a very long time to wash up on shore, but when they do, you never know what can happen.

LEVELS OF AWARENESS AS A WRITER

When I talk to people about my 2021 strategy, I always wonder if it makes sense.

Last year, when I was discussing my sales database project publicly, I received several comments from people in my community who (rightly so) said that they weren't making any money from their books, so there was no reason for them to care about automating their sales.

I tend to do things backward in life. Many of the things I focus on as a writer (particularly data, technology, and the future) are what people start thinking about after they become successful. So I admit that I am a little weird in that regard.

I believe that there are different levels to writing awareness:

- Craft
- Marketing
- Business
- Everything Else

In that order.

When you start your writing journey, you're hyper-focused

on writing craft and productivity. The only thing that matters is starting and finishing your book.

Then your awareness bubble moves outward a little, and you focus on marketing. Once you start making some money, the bubble moves out a little more, and you think about business. Once you've got that under control, then the bubble just keeps moving outward.

Sure, it's not common wisdom, but what would happen if you started instead in reverse? What if you started your awareness as a writer with a keen understanding of where the industry was going, and then narrowed your bubble based on that?

So your awareness bubble would start big and then shrink:

- Everything else (data, technology, and so on)
- Business
- Marketing
- Writing Craft

My personal experience has been that you can get stuck in the writing and marketing awareness bubbles for a long time. Sometimes your ability to have success in those bubbles depends on your awareness of business and everything else.

I also believe that getting stuck in the writing and marketing bubbles will be deadly for writers moving forward, especially in an industry that is ripe for disruption with emerging technology.

THE IDEAL WRITER OF THE FUTURE

I was thinking lately about what the perfect life would look like for a writer. If we could zoom five to ten years into the future and eliminate every problem that a writer faces, what would the ideal writing life look like for the writer of the future?

The ideal writer of the future would never suffer from writer's block. The moment they conceive an idea, they will be able to shepherd it from thought to finished product in record time.

They will be masters of their writing app, unlocking potential that others miss. This will make them more productive and more prolific.

They will be masters of the writing craft.

They will be writing machines, writing book after book with no burnout.

They will be editing machines, using a mix of experience, intuition, technology, and data and analytics to edit their works strategically and in record time.

They will work collaboratively with the right professionals to make their books a reality.

They will publish and manage their books effortlessly,

preferably through seamless integration with their computers and book retailers.

They will use technology to find the right markets for their books so they can sell more books.

They will capitalize on emerging technology to increase their reach, improve their influence, and create a legacy. Artificial intelligence will become a writer's best friend, helping them become a better version of themselves. They will also use these technologies to grow their businesses in their sleep.

That's how I see the ideal writer of the future, and if you think about it, that reality already exists. It's not as ideal in some situations, but writers can do almost everything I described.

That's why this is the greatest time in the history of the world to be a writer. You can start living the future today. All you have to do is know where to look, how to transition your thinking, and how to make strategic gambles. If you can do that, you can step into the future today.

2021 STRATEGY PROGRESS

Last year, I shared my 2021 author strategy, which will guide me for the next several years.

My mission is to educate and entertain my audience in the genres I write, and to remain nimble in an ever-changing industry.

I will achieve my mission through five strategic priorities:

1. Become a world-class content creator
2. Become a world-class marketer
3. Become a technology-driven writer
4. Become a data-driven writer
5. Become the writer of the future

I wanted to give an update on how my progress is going in the first quarter of 2021, and some of the different projects within each of my strategic priorities.

WORLD-CLASS CONTENT CREATOR
Goal: 64 books published by 12/31/2021. I'm

currently at 54 books written (including this one). That means I need to write 10 more books this year.

Develop a way to ensure consistency across my platform. This is just a fancy way of saying that I need to ensure that my work is consistent and that readers are receiving a consistent experience. The editing engine pilot is part of this project—catching routine errors consistently will go a long way toward ensuring a better reader experience, but I'm also thinking about ways to do this across all areas of my platform, such as with my book formatting and my website.

WORLD-CLASS MARKETER

Grow my Amazon Ad imprint. So far, my sales are up by using Amazon Ads.

Improve my copywriting skills. The sales copy builder I discussed in Volume 3 of this series will help me improve my copywriting skills for the books I publish this year.

Reduce my tax liability. I've hired an accountant and we put together a strategy for 2021 to help minimize my taxes this year. I've also grown up and hired a financial advisor, something I was too afraid to do in the past.

BECOME A TECHNOLOGY-DRIVEN WRITER

Develop an automated way to enforce consistency. The editing engine pilot is a good example of this. Using automation, I reduced the number of errors in a manuscript by 34 percent before sending it to an editor. The errors that the editing engine caught will always be caught—it's a permanent, programmatic improvement.

**Redesign my Book Wizard tool on Michael La

Ronn.com and "Author Level Up".com. My goal when people are browsing my website is to get the right books to the right readers at the right time. How can I accomplish that strategically with a blend of automation and technology? I will work on this project later this year.

Implement a flexible book database that houses all the metadata for my books. The goal here is to be able to create an ONIX data feed so that I can publish my books at all retailers with the click of a button in the future when retailers enable this technology for self-published writers. I may not have time for this project.

Automate my bookkeeping. I've talked enough about this topic in this book that I don't need to cover it anymore here.

BECOME A DATA-DRIVEN WRITER

Make minor enhancements to my sales database. I need to continue improving and refining this, and I'll need some programming help.

Invest in learning the basics of Python, Webhooks, and Application Programming Interfaces (APIs). This is good knowledge to understand for the future.

BECOME THE WRITER OF THE FUTURE

Read 50 books. I'm way behind in this area, but I have time to catch up.

Implement direct print and audiobook sales onto my website. No progress here yet, but I do have an audiobook distributor lined up.

Complete my law degree. My last classes end in Q2, so I'm looking forward to being done so I can free up more time to accomplish my other goals in 2021. The legal knowledge I'm gaining will help me in the future.

Complete 12 WMG workshops to improve my writing craft. WMG Workshops are taught by Dean Wesley Smith and Kristine Kathryn Rusch. I haven't taken any yet this year but plan to start in the second quarter. The WMG workshops are writing craft tip extravaganzas.

BRINGING IT ALL TOGETHER

All of the items in this chapter gel together to help me stay nimble.

The fact-checkers and improved research methods I'm experimenting with will make big improvements in the quality of my story.

The content improvements I'm making with my editing engine will make a big difference in the quality of my editing.

The progress I'm making in Amazon Ads and copywriting will help me sell more of my books I write this year.

My adventures with automation, Excel and Word macros, and Natural Language Processing are starting to pay off. I built and deployed up my editing engine pilot in a weekend, whereas this would have taken me weeks if I did it last year because my knowledge base wasn't as strong.

I'm continuing to unlock insights on the data that are hiding in plain sight around me.

And most importantly, I'm keeping my eye on the future.

I'll share more progress on my strategy in the next volume so I can keep myself accountable, but you can view the details of my 2021+ strategy by visiting www.authorlevelup.com/2021s trategy.

IDEAS YOU CAN STEAL

WRITE A PILOT SERIES

In 2014, when I started publishing, I ran an experiment with the small audience I had at the time.

I had four great story ideas, but I couldn't decide which one to write.

The ideas were:

- An urban fantasy with an angel hero
- A post-apocalyptic series about a multigenerational, multicultural family
- A spy technothriller
- A time-travel adventure

Keep in mind my audience was very small, around 25 people. But they voted for the urban fantasy and spy technothriller.

Then I wrote a pilot introduction chapter for both ideas. I shared the pilot chapters with my audience and asked them, "Which one would you want to keep reading?"

The spy series won. That eventually became my *Android X* series. That series went on to do surprisingly well, one of the early bright spots in my early publishing career. It recouped all the costs of editing and cover design in about a year. That was my definition of success back then (and honestly, still is now).

All these years later, I'm thinking about doing it again, but with a twist.

When I did my Amazon Ad experiments late last year, I noticed a trend: the books that performed the best with my ads were books that you could clearly slot into an existing Amazon category.

Some examples of books that did well:

- *The Last Dragon Lord* series (dragons)
- Poetry Collections (Poetry)
- Short Story Collection (Short Story Anthologies)

Some examples of books that did not perform well (initially):

- My urban fantasy about a dream mage
- My urban fantasy about a necromancer

It's not that dream mages or necromancers are bad ideas. This isn't an indictment on the books. However, Amazon struggled to serve them to similar books without a lot of work from me. It's not used to looking for necromancer books because that character type is off-market right now.

So I had an idea that you can steal: what if I wrote two pilot chapters for two completely different series, asked my existing fiction audience to read and vote for which one they'd like to keep reading, and then:

- pay for professional covers for both stories as if they were novels

- have both chapters professionally edited
- publish both introductory chapters on Amazon for free or $0.99, and put them in Kindle Unlimited
- pretend that each title is a real book and support it with the proper keywords, a strong book description, and so on.
- optimize the book description by explaining that this is an exploratory pilot and that the book that wins will become a full series.
- End the book with a call to action to click if they like the book, as well as a link to the other book and a request to join my mailing list.

Then (and here's what makes this an interesting idea) I would run Amazon Ads to both pilots to see what happens.

When the experiment was over, I would have solid data points.

- Which pilot did my existing audience like the best, and why?
- Which pilot had the best ad performance? Did the Amazon Sponsored Product Automatic ads turn on? If yes, that's an indicator that Amazon could find comparable titles. If no, it's an indicator that there's something off-market about the book.
- What are the comparable titles for the book as revealed by the ad search term reports?
- How does the ad data compare to my existing audience's preferences? Do they want the same thing?

As you can see, this is like the exercise I did in 2014, but it's supported by data.

There are caveats, though. First, Amazon is not the whole world. It's one retailer out of many, and the ads would primarily be run in the United States. US readers are not a barometer of other countries, so that's a downside. However, I could run ads in the United Kingdom, Canada, and Australia too, but that doesn't completely solve the problem.

Second, trends change over time. The ad data is just a snapshot in time. The "loser" pilot shouldn't be viewed as a loser at all.

Third, this depends entirely on my execution. Both pilots would need to be alpha-read, beta-read, and professionally edited and proofread. I'd also need to invest in professional covers for both pilots, covers that would be *final*. So that would be an investment. But is it worth it to spend a few hundred dollars for the chance to net three to four figures each month for the foreseeable future? At this stage in my career, I can afford the risk, though it would sting if I failed.

But hey, that's why ideas exist—for us to prove whether they work or not!

INDIE AUTHOR AI CO-AUTHOR
COLLECTIVE

As I think about artificial intelligence, I'm constantly reminded of how much data you need to get meaningful results.

This will probably be true with using AI to write books. Until AI engines can do more with less data, you would need a LOT of books for an AI to write in your author's voice.

Traditional publishers could easily build a corpus of data by adding their entire backlog into an AI system. Self-published writers will lack that ability.

However, a group of self-published writers in the same genre could band together, feed all of their books into an AI engine, and then use that as the corpus for new artificially-generated books. The books would be derivative works based on the authors' books. The authors could then publish under a pseudonym that suggests AI, such as "James Urban.AI" for urban fantasy. Then the authors could publish the book, co-market it, and split the royalties.

Imagine if 100 prolific indie authors did this in a genre. It would be a smart way to fight back in the AI battle that is almost certain to come: traditional publishers of the future, who will use artificial intelligence and data and analytics as the basis for their insights and publishing decisions, versus self-publishers, who have almost no data and analytics other than their own.

HIRING AN AUDIOBOOK PROOFER

I read a great guest blog post on "The Creative Penn" written by Max Cantrell, who is an audiobook proof listener. Just as you'd hire an editor to check your work for errors, Max is the guy you'd hire to listen to your audiobook for errors such as misspellings, mispronunciations, or noise artifacts in your narrator's recording.

A unique problem with audiobook creation is comparing the narration with the text to make sure they match. You'd be surprised how many times a narrator will accidentally skip a word or pronounce a word incorrectly, almost always unconsciously. I once had a narrator say a person's last name correctly in one sentence and mispronounce it in the very next sentence. Even the best narrators might sometimes bump the table they're recording at, or their chair might squeak, or a background noise might show up in the recording. Narrators usually catch most of these artifacts, but not even the best can catch them all.

To produce a quality audiobook, it needs to be free of mispronunciations, missing words and phrases, and artifacts. The text needs to match the audio exactly.

Yet when I listen to my audiobook proofs, I don't like to sit in front of my computer and compare it to the text. It's mind-numbing, time-consuming work. If you have a 10-hour audiobook, it'll take you *at least* 10 hours to perform this task, likely more because you'll have to start and stop a lot to make notes. If you want to do this right, you have to do it twice—once to give the narrator a list of errors, and then again to make sure the narrator didn't make any additional mistakes while fixing the original errors.

I prefer to be multi-tasking when I listen to proof audio, because that's how most listeners are going to be consuming the book. I'm mostly listening for flow and quality. I prefer to do the text and audio comparison second.

It's a pretty smart idea to hire someone who can handle the comparison for you and give you a list of errors with timestamps that you can pass to your narrator. It serves as an additional layer of protection to ensure that you're creating a quality product.

While I recommend that you check out Max's services, I predict he has a lot of clients at this point. This is a job you can easily hire a freelancer to do on a site like Upwork or Fiverr. Simply pay them per finished hour of your audiobook, which might (at the time of this writing) be anywhere from $20 to $30 per finished hour. A 10-hour audiobook would cost you $200, which is what you would pay a *good* narrator *per finished hour*. This is a perfect job for a freelancer just starting who wants to build a portfolio.

I intend to use an audio proofer moving forward. It's a cost-effective way to improve the presentation of your content. Once you publish an audiobook, it's fairly permanent, so it pays to get it right the first time.

CLEVER DICTATION HACK

I stumbled upon a clever dictation hack that I'd like to pass along to anyone who is disheartened by the fact that Dragon for Mac has been discontinued.

Recently, I did a Writing Power Hour Livestream and wanted to dictate live so that my audience could see how I did it. I needed a way to share my screen.

I had two problems. The first problem was that I use Dragon on my Windows virtual machine, which I cannot share if I am screen sharing on my Mac. The virtual machine consumes too many resources and would jeopardize my stream quality. It's a big no-no.

The second problem was that I needed to share my dictation on-screen.

I decided to use Dragon Anywhere on my phone. Could I somehow get my phone's display onto my desktop monitor? Why, yes, I could, using the iPhone's "screen mirroring" feature. I downloaded a $17 app called Reflector that accepted the screen mirroring stream and displayed it on my Mac. Then I shared my screen, and voila! I could dictate with my phone on my desk but see the results on my computer screen.

(Android phones support screen mirroring too, and you can use Reflector with them.)

So if you have a Mac and want to use Dragon, purchase a Dragon Anywhere subscription and take the steps I just described. It's not perfect, and you don't receive all the benefits of the Windows desktop version of Dragon, but you can dictate like everyone else and achieve very good results. In my opinion, Dragon Anywhere is almost as accurate as Dragon for Desktop, and you don't need special hardware.

METADATA CONSULTANT

There are many author services for self-published authors, including people who help with marketing.

However, I have (personally) not seen anyone specifically hold themselves out as a metadata consultant, especially for Amazon.

Picking the right keywords and categories on Amazon is critical. It's an ever-changing battle.

Someone who reviewed your book and helped you pick the right keywords and categories is an underrated service idea in my opinion. Especially if that person did this service all day every day. I've attended webinars with SEO consultants who talk about their process for picking the right metadata for a book. I would love to pay someone with that kind of mind to look at my books and offer advice I hadn't considered. It's easy to pick bad keywords, and you don't always know how to fix it.

A metadata consultant could also add value by reviewing your sales data and Amazon Ad performance to help you determine whether your keywords need adjusting. You can pay them an hourly fee for their help, or purchase a "maintenance package," in which they check in with you a couple of times a year to see if trends have changed.

The key is that this person must specialize in Amazon SEO. Anyone can claim to do this, but Amazon SEO knowledge is a special skill set.

GENRE CONSULTANT

Some readers are masters of their genre. These readers have read every single book in a subgenre, and they buy new releases on day one. They've read it all.

What would it be like to tap in to these readers' knowledge and experience? Book 30 minutes with "Dan the Space Man," who has an encyclopedic knowledge of space opera. Let him read the first three or four chapters of your book and tell you what it reminds him of.

"This is like that one novel in the 1970s by X author," Dan might say. Or, "It's like that, but it reads like X author."

If Dan says, "I've never seen anything like this before," that's probably a red flag. You shouldn't be able to stump him.

A thirty-minute conversation with Dan would give you a list of comparable books, an understanding of where the major tropes of your story compare to other books in the genre, and an understanding of some potential pitfalls. He could also tell you what to put on the cover to appeal to readers like him. This is, of course, one person's opinion, but my experience with readers has been that if one person says something, there are many more who believe it.

"Dan the Space Man" is a super reader, but also what you could call a genre consultant. Many successful writers have a good understanding of the genres they write in, but they don't have the time to read everything. Writers who write to market could use Dan's expertise too.

You can hire editors who have expertise in a genre, and while that is helpful, there's nothing like getting opinions from readers.

BOOK COVER HUNTER

What do you want on your book cover? I don't know about you, but I often struggle with coming up with a concept of what should be on the cover. The designer usually needs a basic idea to start from.

What if there was a way for you to feed images of book covers into an engine (maybe artificial intelligence-driven), and the engine would find similar book covers and return them to you?

You can (sort of) do this with Google Images reverse search feature. You can upload an image and Google will return visually similar images, mostly based on the color palette.

I envision something more powerful and targeted that can identify whether an image is a book cover and whether the cover is potentially in your genre. It could also "hunt" for similar images, crawling Amazon, Pinterest, and Google at the same time to give you a more comprehensive search. It would be an exceptional market research tool.

Combine this with the genre consultant I mentioned earlier and you'll have a recipe for a book that hits the market with both content and packaging.

STUDYING READER HABITS

I heard an interview with an influencer in the self-publishing space who talked about hiring a firm to do a marketing study where they tracked how readers browse for books on Amazon. They tracked the users' screens and paid careful attention to how they navigated Amazon and where they spent the most time on a product page. The insights were intriguing.

How interesting would it be if the authors of a subgenre got together and commissioned a similar study, but for other things? Show readers a bunch of book covers in rapid succession and see what draws their attention first, then ask them why they clicked. Or, show them different varieties of back matter and track how they engage with it to see if there's a particular style of a call to action that works best. Or, simply track users' screens to see how they search for urban fantasy novels, for example, to see if there are genre-specific quirks that authors need to know about.

I have no idea what a service like this would cost, but there is so much data out there waiting to be discovered.

MARKETING WORKBENCH

There are so many marketing tools for writers that it might be helpful to bring them under one umbrella. For example, I've mentioned several different tools in the *Indie Author Confidential* series that could exist in one place. Imagine an app or a website with the following tools:

BOOK COVERS

- A "book cover hunter," which hunts down book covers similar to yours
- A font dissector that can analyze a book cover and tell you what the fonts are
- A font list with the most common fonts broken down by genre, with trending data
- A report driven by AI that informs authors what's happening with book covers in the genre

BOOK DESCRIPTIONS

- A book description builder that helps you build a solid book description every time
- A copywriting swipe file

MARKETING

- Integration with a link localization service to help you build marketing links
- Integration with a social media scheduler
- A brand monitoring tool

These tools are mostly unrelated to each other, but it would be nice to access them in one place, or at least be able to link to them so that authors could go to one place to find the tools they need.

GENRE-BASED MUSIC

I discovered some new music by an artist I like on Apple Music. Several of the songs had a similar theme: supernatural love. The lyrics were mystical, mysterious, and fun. That got me thinking about what an interesting partnership a bestselling author could strike with a bestselling musician.

Here's an example of the idea: urban fantasy rock. A band records an album that is essentially urban fantasy short stories put to music: what it's like to be a werewolf, a man falling in love with a ghost woman, a treasure hunter fighting off ghouls in a temple in Peru, and so on. Pair *au courant*, top-notch musicality that fans of the (music) genre love with content that fans of a (book) genre love. You can tell a fascinating story and cover a lot of ground in just three verses and a chorus.

And if you'd like an example of what this could sound like, listen to a 1984 classic by Dave Grusin and Randy Goodrum called "Haunting Me."

Imagine yacht-rock romance, LitRPG electronica, literary jazz, epic fantasy songs sung in made-up languages, and so on. There are a lot of pairings you can explore when you explore demographics too.

There would be lucrative partnership opportunities between authors and artists working in the same genre, even cross-promotion and licensing opportunities. For example, the band could license a character to do an album from the character's perspective, or the author could make the band characters in one of their novels.

INFLUENCER DIRECT PLATFORM

I discussed in a previous chapter how I chatted with a developer about creating a dedicated app on which people could consume my content. I loved the idea but ultimately didn't pursue it.

If you think about this and apply next-order thinking, it becomes difficult for end-users to manage. Imagine if every influencer in the world had a dedicated app that served their content. If you follow 10 influencers, that's 10 apps you'd have to install on your phone, all with different features and functionality. That will never work.

Here's what could: a white-label app that allows influencers to upload their content in the same structure and format. Users merely "search" for influencers to follow in the app, and once they click follow, the influencer's content appears in the app's feed, and the user can also follow the influencer directly. It would be similar to a social media app, but it would allow direct engagement with the influencer as well as a community. It would be a more intimate way for influencers to serve their content. So in a sense, you're downloading one app and then choosing which influencers to follow within that app. Influencers would pay premium prices to get in, and the app would offer features that would be almost identical to a custom app solution, but for a more affordable price. The app would have a name like "Chasr: The App That Lets You Keep Up with the Influencers Who Matter Most." Something like that. Unlike social media apps, Chasr wouldn't encourage native content. It would instead serve content that exists on the channels, such as YouTube, a podcast, or a blog. All an influencer would need to do is *syndicate* their existing content to it. I can't stress this enough. Otherwise, the app becomes just like every social media app out there.

It seems to me that users want to interact with their favorite influencers more intimately, but they don't necessarily want to download an app for that one person unless they are fanatic about that influencer. Even then, it's doubtful that they would use *one person's app every single day* because of convenience.

PUBLISHING CONTENT CURATION SERVICE

For years, enemies of self-publishing decried the "tsunami of crap" that self-published books ushered onto the market. You don't hear that term very much anymore, but God, it was everywhere in 2010-2014. I don't miss that term. I never liked it.

But since we're talking about tsunamis, why don't we instead talk about the tsunami of information that exists about self-publishing? Ever since 2010ish, authors have had to navigate a never-ending amount of information on how to be a better author, marketer, and businessperson. There are services such as "The Hot Sheet" by Jane Friedman and *The Writer's Knowledge Base* by Elizabeth Spann Craig that curate self-publishing knowledge and each of these services is great in their own way. But there is no single service that I know of that can capture *everything*.

Eight years ago, I would have recommended that someone do this manually, but even a full-time curator would be embarking on a fool's errand. These days, I believe artificial intelligence can solve the problem. An AI can consume blog posts, books, podcasts, YouTube videos, and even comments on social media and contextualize them.

So many news articles these days are written and created by artificial intelligence, so AI already has the capability to consume content and create context. If it can do that, then it can also organize and recommend content based on what you are looking for, and aim to recommend the "right content to the right user at the right time."

Imagine wanting to know the hottest marketing trends. The service could spin a narrative about what people are doing right now based on recent content. It could even spin you a narrative based on how a certain marketing technique has evolved, such as Amazon Ads. As such, it might be able to warn you about certain practices that are either out of favor or no longer effective.

Simply ask your Amazon Alexa device "What's the self-publishing news?" And you'd get a daily 10-minute report broken into different industry segments such as traditional publishing, self-publishing, marketing, Facebook advertising, and so on. You might even get a highlights reel from the most popular self-publishing podcasts, with snippets that you might want to hear.

This could work on any device, not just Amazon Echos.

The curation service can help you navigate the tsunami and find knowledge too.

Imagine wanting to learn how to format a book. An AI would recommend to you the most up-to-date information based on context clues such as screenshots of the apps used and social engagement (users aren't complaining about the posts being out of date, for example), among other things. If you're using Scrivener for Windows to format a book, you'll receive Scrivener for Windows content. The engine might even flag certain articles if it thinks portions of them are out of date. The genius of an engine like this is that while it's likely to recommend popular content, the primary goal would be to recommend the *right* content based on what the user is searching for, which means that it could pull up obscure blog posts from lesser-known locales if they're the right thing for the user.

The future belongs to those who can crack the discoverability problem.

CONTENT CREATED WHILE WRITING THIS BOOK

Author Level Up YouTube Channel - Highlights

Watch at youtube.com/authorlevelup.

The Ultimate Guide to Book Editing (series): Watch the concepts that Michael talks about in this book in action.

How to Beat Self-Doubt as a Writer: Learn how to conquer self-doubt forever.

Interviews & Appearances

Be a Writing Machine (Writer's Digest Conference 2020): Discover Michael's secrets for being insanely productive, and how he wrote over 50 books while working a full-time job, raising a family, and attending law school classes in the evenings. This talk is based on Michael's top selling book, *Be a Writing Machine.*

How to Create Engaging Characters (GDEX 2020 Conference): In this presentation, Michael talks about his process for creating engaging characters that readers will love.

Mental Models for Writers (Escape from the Plot Forest Summit 2020): In this talk, Michael explains the power of mental models and how writers can use them to level up in every area of their life—especially writing their stories!

READ THE NEXT VOLUME

Michael's writer journey continues in the next volume of this series!

Grab your copy at www.authorlevelup.com/confidential.

MEET M.L. RONN

Science fiction and fantasy on the wild side!

M.L. Ronn (Michael La Ronn) is the author of many science fiction and fantasy novels including *The Good Necromancer*, *Android X*, and *The Last Dragon Lord* series.

In 2012, a life-threatening illness made him realize that storytelling was his #1 passion. He's devoted his life to writing ever since, making up whatever story makes him fall out of his chair laughing the hardest. Every day.

Learn more about Michael
www.authorlevelup.com (for writers)
www.michaellaronn.com (fiction)

MORE BOOKS BY M.L. RONN

Books for Writers:

www.authorlevelup.com/books

Fiction:
www.michaellaronn.com/books